For Jack and Mary McCall,
Two Who Embody the Spirit of Paideia.

The Power of Paideia Schools:
Defining Lives Through Learning

INTRODUCTION

William Chesser, Michael Hale, and Terry Roberts

In the title of a March 1984 article in *Educational Leadership*, Dennis Gray, an original member of the Paideia Group, asked rhetorically, "Whatever Became of Paideia?" He went on to question whether the original Paideia Group had delivered "an idea whose time [had] not yet come" (p. 56). True reform based on the Paideia model, Gray admitted, is time-consuming and uncomfortable. And, because Paideia is about "learning to act differently, not just talk differently" about schooling, he even predicted a 10-year implementation process.

Despite the enthusiasm of educators like Gray, Albert Shanker, and Ted Sizer (who incorporated many of the Paideia ideas into the principles of the Coalition of Essential Schools), the Paideia program did not immediately translate into successful projects. Even with the establishment of the National Paideia Center (NPC) at the University of North Carolina in 1988, the program did not spawn a network of Paideia schools until several years later. In 1992 a new staff brought a new approach—working in close, classroom-based partnership with schools—to the National Paideia Center, and the results have been dramatic. The center is currently working with more than 40 schools in 12 states, and the list grows monthly. The question that lurks at the heart of this brief history is, Why did a program that seemed to have fallen into a decade of dormancy suddenly spring back to life?

The first reason is that the original Paideia principles are an elegant condensation of the best thinking about public education. In language that is spare and powerful, the original Paideia Group captured both the need for serious school reform and the profound connection between school reform and the United States as a functional democracy. For the first time in a generation, *The Paideia Proposal* (Adler, 1982) boldly stated a litany of principles that have become all but schoolhouse verities. Such principles as "all children can learn" and "therefore they deserve the same quality, not just quantity, of education" undergird many of the reform proposals of recent years. It is important to remember that the *Proposal* predated *A Nation at Risk* (National Commission on Excellence in Education, 1983) by only a few months and profoundly affected the heated debates that *A Nation at Risk* precipitated. It is difficult to name a leading educational reform program that has not been demonstrably influenced by Paideia principles, and local educators throughout the United States now openly embrace what in 1982 seemed radical ideas.

This brings us to the second, and perhaps more important, reason why interest in Paideia has grown so rapidly over the last few years. The Paideia principles successfully marry a fundamentally conservative idea—the beneficial rigors of a classical education—and a fundamentally liberal one—progressive teaching and learning practices. Nel Noddings, Diane Ravitch, and others have pointed out that what Adler prescribes in the Paideia program is a synthesis of Robert Hutchins's call for a return to classical education and John Dewey's progressivist ideas about learning.[1] These seemingly contradictory ideas—intellectual rigor and equal access to a quality education—have become the bedrock upon which successful Paideia schools are built. This synthesis of conservative and liberal ideas is important because, as education reform has become more intensely politicized over the past decade, parents and teachers have discovered in Paideia a comprehensive and *apolitical* design. We advocate for well-defined and rigorous standards in a core curriculum, and we work hard at helping local educators adapt a classical model to their needs. At the same time, we stress the absolute need to make American public education more democratic through more heterogeneous grouping, creative scheduling, and teaching practices that engage the interests and abilities of all students.

---

[1]See Noddings's 1992 book, *The Challenge to Care in Schools*, and Ravitch's 1983 reply to *The Paideia Proposal* in the *Harvard Educational Review*. Interestingly, Noddings takes Adler to task specifically for merging Hutchins and Dewey, arguing that "Dewey disagreed with Robert Hutchins and Mortimer Adler on what the best and wisest parents would want for their children" (p. 44). Ravitch, on the other hand, praises Adler's synthesis of the two.

Perhaps the most important reasons for Paideia's resurgence are that the program now includes all subjects and embraces important texts from diverse cultures. In the chapters that follow, we will provide practical information on how to use the principles of Paideia in mathematics, science, music, literature, writing, physical education—all the subjects in the core curriculum. Examples of seminar texts will include powerful examples of classics, some contemporary, by African American, Hispanic, Asian, and other writers, as well as authors commonly associated with the classical tradition. Our bedrock beliefs in excellent materials and rigorous study are never violated, but Hutchins's "great conversation" is expanded to include all the core subjects and the rich cultural diversity that is the United States.

There is no contradiction in the Paideia program's advocacy of a classical education for all American students and inclusion of selected innovative teaching techniques. Research on such techniques as project learning, cooperative learning, writing across the curriculum, and seminar instruction makes it clear that we can both demand more sophisticated intellectual work from students and at the same time engage a much wider range of students in that work. Dramatically enhancing performance requires that we both demand more of students and simultaneously teach them well. Neither tactic alone is enough.

A Classical Education

In 1952 Robert Hutchins wrote a landmark description and argument in favor of what he termed a "liberal education." In his essay, "The Great Conversation," Hutchins contended that the classical works of Western thought constituted one long conversation in which men and women from successive ages wrestled with the myriad problems of humanity. These works, he maintained, should be read as part of a conversation rather than as independent statements because traditionally an educated man or woman was steeped in classical expression and would construct his or her own response to the world in the context of what had been said and done before. Hutchins's original use of the term *conversation* referred to this ongoing dialogue of ideas "that began in the dawn of history and continues to this day," consisting of the "great works of the mind" in print, in the arts, and in music (pp. 1–2).

Paideia schools have expanded on Hutchins's definition of conversation in two important ways. First, any active learner in a Paideia school carries on a dialogue with an author when he or she interacts with a book, a work of art, or a musical composition, weighing and considering not only the artist's message but also the assumptions and implications of that message and whether it is factually or conceptually valid. Second, Paideia schools prescribe in detail how an active learner can best converse with a text through formal discussion with a group of fellow students. The key learning event in a Paideia classroom is often a formalized teaching technique known as the Paideia seminar, in which students examine a text in-depth, first articulating their ideas in response to it and then working to justify and clarify their ideas. Here the use of conversation is obvious: The seminar participant must actively listen, think, and speak—offering opinions and asking questions—on what often become quite abstract topics. And as Mortimer Adler, who defined the seminar in the early 1980s, was careful to point out, the purpose of this teaching technique is to make students grapple with the ideas and values inherent in a body of information, specifically in the text at hand.

The classics should inform the education of all students because they are by definition the repository of any culture's best thought and most profound feeling about the human condition. When Hutchins writes of what he terms the "liberal education," an education steeped in the great works of a culture, he says clearly that "the aim of liberal education is human excellence, both private and public" (p. 3). He means that virtue, generosity, and right action are the ultimate goals of schooling, not just employability or high test scores. He goes on to write that

> the liberally educated man is at home in the world of ideas and in the world of practical affairs, too, because he understands the relation of the two. . . . He may even derive from his liberal education some conception of the difference between a bad world and a good one and some notion of the ways in which one might be turned into the other. (p. 4)

The classical curriculum is built, then, on a rigorous study of a culture's foundation documents and has as its goal a rich, full adult life for all students. It is "basic" in the sense that it is our common heritage.

The frequently heard contemporary argument against reading and discussing the classics, however, centers around the danger represented by limiting access to the dialogue through the classics teachers choose to teach. When E. D. Hirsch first proposed the necessity for *Cultural Literacy* in his 1987 book by that title, he included a list of "What Every American Should Know." Although this was not a reading list per se, it was culturally biased, and Hirsch drew the same sort of fire that was directed at Mortimer Adler and others who published reading lists. Hirsch's critics argued that his notion of culture was filtered through a narrow Anglo-Saxon male lens that precluded many of the multiple cultures that make up the United States. Hirsch denied these charges, and he and his colleagues expanded their various "lists" in subsequent books. The debate between mono- and multiculturalism goes on (as it should); but more to the point is Hirsch's candid assessment of the political, social, and economic power of a classical education:

> Literate culture is the most democratic culture in our land: it excludes nobody; it cuts across generations and social groups and classes; it is not usually one's first culture, but it should be everyone's second, existing as it does beyond the narrow spheres of family, neighborhood, and region. (p. 21)

The compelling point here is that reading introduces any child to a fascinating universe of thought and feeling beyond the local, and that despite our diverse backgrounds, we can all hold that universe in common.

The common ground of literate culture is where individuals of vastly disparate backgrounds can meet peacefully—or at least they can if that common ground is extensive enough. As Hutchins was careful to point out, "no age speaks with a single voice" (p. 9), and any effort to define culture too narrowly defeats the purpose of civilized dialogue. For that reason, students must encounter in a profound way Lao Tzu's *Tao te Ching* as well as Machiavelli's *The Prince*, and Zora Neale Hurston's *Their Eyes Were Watching God* as well as Euripides' *Medea*, first performed 25 centuries ago.

We must define culture broadly enough to engage the hearts and minds of our students without giving in to the urge to substitute superficial current works for timeless ones.

In a world that grows progressively smaller and more violent, we need now more than ever the ability to consider opposing ideas in a civilized way. One can only hope that Hutchins is right when he argues that

> the goal toward which Western society moves is the civilization of the Dialogue. The spirit of Western civilization is the spirit of inquiry. Its dominant element is the *logos*. Nothing is to remain undiscussed. Everybody is to speak his mind. No proposition is to be left unexamined. (p. 1)

It is easy to take Hutchins to task for limiting his vision to "Western civilization" when the 21st century will certainly see the collision and confusion of the many world cultures. His call for dialogue wherein "everybody is to speak his [or her] mind," however, only becomes more urgent as our planet grows smaller and more fragile.

As we have come to define it in Paideia reform, "classical" involves far more than rejoining Hutchins's great conversation. It also involves the return to a core curriculum of integrated subjects, an ambitious mastery of "basic" skills, and teaching to a rare depth of understanding for all students. In *The Paideia Proposal*, Adler and the Paideia Group advocated not only a universal emphasis on math, science, language arts, and social studies but also a consistent engagement in physical health, fine arts (including music), and foreign language. The current standards movement in the United States has reawakened the debate over which of the traditional subject areas should constitute the "core" of a universal curriculum; and in Paideia schools we fight to maintain movement, art, music, and language as essential and to integrate their study and practice into that of the "academic" subjects.

A second facet of classical education as we define it is the expanded notion of what should constitute the basic skills of a successful student. Surprisingly, the business community, educators dedicated to preparing future citizens, and proponents of lifelong learning often agree on what those skills are. The 1991 SCANS (Secretary's Commission on Achieving Necessary Skills) report listed various skills and qualities in a Three-Part Foundation for preparation of the ideal future work force (see fig. I.1).

FIGURE I.1
A Three-Part Foundation

Basic Skills: Reads, writes, performs arithmetic and mathematical operations, listens, and speaks

A. *Reading*—locates, understands, and interprets written information in prose and in documents such as manuals, graphs, and schedules

B. *Writing*—communicates thoughts, ideas, information, and messages in writing; and creates documents such as letters, directions, manuals, reports, graphs, and flowcharts

C. *Arithmetic/Mathematics*—performs basic computations and approaches practical problems by choosing appropriately from a variety of mathematical techniques

D. *Listening*—receives, attends to, interprets, and responds to verbal messages and other cues

E. *Speaking*—organizes ideas and communicates orally

Thinking Skills: Thinks creatively, makes decisions, solves problems, visualizes, knows how to learn, and reasons

A. *Creative Thinking*—generates new ideas

B. *Decision Making*—specifies goals and constraints, generates alternatives, considers risks, and evaluates and chooses best alternative

C. *Problem Solving*—recognizes problems and devises and implements a plan of action

D. *Seeing Things in the Mind's Eye*—organizes, and processes symbols, pictures, graphs, objects, and other information

E. *Knowing How to Learn*—uses efficient learning techniques to acquire and apply new knowledge and skills

F. *Reasoning*—discovers a rule or principle underlying the relationship between two or more objects and applies it when solving a problem

Personal Qualities: Displays responsibility, self-esteem, sociability, self-management, and integrity and honesty

A. *Responsibility*—exerts a high level of effort and perseveres toward goal attainment

B. *Self-Esteem*—believes in own self-worth and maintains a positive view of self

C. *Sociability*—demonstrates understanding, friendliness, adaptability, empathy, and politeness in group settings

D. *Self-Management*—assesses self accurately, sets personal goals, monitors progress, and exhibits self-control

E. *Integrity/Honesty*—chooses ethical courses of action

Interestingly, the same characteristics are an equally valid description—according to Paideia standards—of the ideal future citizen and lifelong learner. The fundamental emphasis on broad-ranging skills in communications, problem solving, and teamwork is so compelling that such skills have become, along with literacy and mathematics, the new basics in education. One can argue (as did Hutchins, among others) that a classical education is the best vocational preparation for all students but only if it teaches children to "think creatively, make decisions, [and] solve problems."

The pedagogical reply to the challenge represented by the SCANS report lies in Adler's three columns of instruction, which consist of didactic instruction, intellectual coaching, and Socratic seminars (see fig. I.2). In this model, students constantly practice the "necessary skills" while engaged in producing relevant products of real-world value.

If a rigorous core curriculum and the mastery of intellectual skills are the first two characteristics of a classical education, the third is a complementary emphasis on the ability to analyze, synthesize, and evaluate the validity of ideas. Using Adler's third column, the Paideia seminar, as the capstone of most units of study allows Paideia schools to consistently require students to practice higher-order thinking skills in an organized and rigorous fashion. In a Paideia school, then, the term "classical education" has wide-ranging implications—for intellectual standards and curriculum reform as well as teacher behavior and student learning.

The Essential Elements

A template for the 21st century model of classical education was created in 1992–93. Called the "Essential Elements of a Paideia School," it describes in practical terms a fully realized Paideia school. If the original Paideia Group's well-known list of 12 Principles symbolizes the paradigm shift in values and philosophy that must accompany true school improvement, the 14 Essential Elements provide the blueprint for realizing how those values and philosophy might translate into the real world of public schooling—education as the students experience it.

FIGURE I.2
Three Columns of Instruction

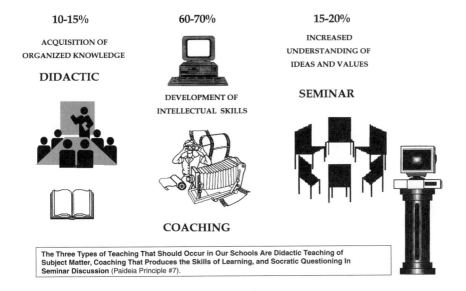

10-15%	60-70%	15-20%
ACQUISITION OF ORGANIZED KNOWLEDGE		INCREASED UNDERSTANDING OF IDEAS AND VALUES
DIDACTIC	DEVELOPMENT OF INTELLECTUAL SKILLS	**SEMINAR**
	COACHING	

The Three Types of Teaching That Should Occur in Our Schools Are Didactic Teaching of Subject Matter, Coaching That Produces the Skills of Learning, and Socratic Questioning In Seminar Discussion (Paideia Principle #7).

This document came about because teachers and principals demanded more concrete guidance in implementing the Paideia program. Significantly, it emerged from a months-long, collaborative writing process. Multiple drafts of the document were circulated to educators around the country who had implemented various aspects of Paideia education. Thus it is written by practitioners as well as theorists, intended to be used by principals, teachers, and parents in moving from the ideal vision of school reform to the real world of teachers and children. These Essential Elements, accompanied by concrete, practical examples from all types of schools and from all subject areas, constitute the bulk of this book.

The first section of the Essential Elements, entitled General Characteristics, describes the context that both insulates and nurtures high-quality teaching and learning. The six elements in this section (discussed in Chapter 1) show how students can learn to accept responsibility for their own behavior and learning in the context of a larger community dedicated to lifelong education. In addition, Elements 3 through 5 describe the important roles that adults involved in a Paideia school must assume as model learners and cooperating teachers. Element 6 addresses the need for marshaling community resources to aid families so that all children can come to the classroom ready and able to learn. In general, each of the first six elements has to do with creating a learning community both within the school and in the larger world outside the school.

The second section of the Essential Elements, Teaching Strategies and Techniques (described in Chapters 2 through 4), refers to the three columns of Paideia teaching and learning strategies. In many ways, these three elements are the heart and soul of a Paideia school because they have to do with the relationship between teacher and student. Implementation of Paideia in an individual classroom typically takes several years as teachers first master seminar leadership and then integrate seminars into fully developed three-column units of study. Successful schoolwide implementation of all three elements often requires two to three years.

Elements 10 through 12 (explored in Chapters 5 through 7) make up the third section, entitled Curriculum Issues. This section most clearly defines our emphasis on intellectual rigor in a core curriculum. Elements 10 and 12 directly address the need to engage students across a wide range of learning styles and intelligences within the framework of a common core. Element 11 suggests how student learning should drive all other elements of school structure (specifically scheduling).

The last two elements—discussed in Chapter 8, Assessment—deal with evaluation and emphasize the need for individual assessment of both student and teacher progress. They make up the last section of the Essential Elements. Paideia philosophy stresses the primary role of teachers as model learners, whose ongoing work is evident both in their individual classrooms and in the school at large. The assessment process for students and adults alike should be both demanding and fluid, and it should address a full range of knowledge, skills, and understanding of ideas.

Taken together, the 14 Essential Elements of a Paideia School represent an imposing design. They challenge nearly every aspect of public school structure and behavior. To echo Dennis Gray, they require that teachers, parents, and children "learn to act differently, not just talk differently" about schooling. One need only visit the schools described in this book (see Appendix B), however, to see that universal rigor in a public school is possible. And one need only visit the "average" public school in the United States to see that it is urgently, profoundly needed.

A CLASSICAL EDUCATION FOR THE 21ST CENTURY

Terry Roberts

The Paideia school is student centered and, as a result, involves students in governance and expects all students to succeed. Administrators and teachers model lifelong learning because the school cares about the intellectual development of both students and adults. Finally, the school becomes the center of a larger learning community.

The Paideia school is defined by intellectual rigor for all students. Both challenging and democratic, it teaches all students a common core curriculum in predominantly heterogeneous groups. To realistically target high achievement for all students, however, the Paideia school must be a student-centered school in several significant ways. It honors the progressive traditions established by John Dewey by creating active environments in classrooms and by giving students authentic work to do. And while the Paideia school emphasizes learning, the adults who work there understand the central role that caring plays in honoring students and their work; they understand, in other words, that a humane environment nurtures learning.

In an article in *Educational Researcher*, Linda Darling-Hammond (1996) describes the dilemma facing public education when she argues that we must focus

> on developing the potential of each individual to a high extent, a critical mission for a pluralistic society with increasing needs for talent development. Such powerful teaching and learning require schools that value and evaluate serious intellectual performances, that support responsive teaching, and that allow teachers to build strong, long-term relationships with

students and their parents. If we cannot build such schools at this moment in history, I believe that a deeply stratified society—one divided by access to knowledge and the opportunity to learn—could undo our chances for democratic life and government. (p. 7)

A Return to Classical Education

It is in response to precisely this difficult, multifaceted challenge that Paideia educators propose a return to what we are calling a "classical" education. The term *classical* itself is controversial because of the elitist, Eurocentric, and paternalistic connotations it carries; but given the Paideia definition of the word, it may well be the only viable educational alternative for the 21st century American public school.

For our purposes, *classical* means

- Overt attention to and participation in Robert Hutchins's "Great Conversation" (1952), the cultural heritage of all our children;
- A rigorous common core curriculum of integrated subjects;
- An ambitious mastery of fundamental skills in communication, computation, teamwork, and problem solving; and
- Learning to a depth of intellectual understanding often missing in our schools.

Furthermore, it means that all these characteristics should define the learning life of *every* child. These are, obviously, ambitious goals—ambitious, but necessarily so in light of the profound challenges described by Darling-Hammond.

The original Paideia principles, constructed by Mortimer Adler and the Paideia Group in the early 1980s, listed "three callings for which schooling should prepare all Americans":

1. To earn a decent livelihood
2. To be a good citizen of the nation and the world
3. To make a good life for one's self (National Paideia Center, 1988).

If the third calling seems ambiguous, perhaps the clue to its meaning can be found in one other primary principle:

> that schooling at its best is preparation for becoming generally educated in the course of a whole lifetime, and that schools should be judged on how well they provide such preparation. (National Paideia Center, 1988)

If there is a way to eliminate the danger of the disastrously stratified society described by Darling-Hammond, it is employability, citizenship, and a life defined by learning—not for some but for all. The classical or, as Hutchins terms it, "liberal" education recognizes the same goals:

> the aim of liberal education is human excellence, both private and public. . . . The liberally educated man [or woman] is at home in the world of ideas and in the world of practical affairs, too, because he [or she] understands the relation of the two. (pp. 3–4)

A classical education empowers the individual by providing the tools necessary to not only survive but thrive in the volatile world of the 21st century.

What kinds of schools are capable of empowering by teaching a stunningly wide range of students, raising all to a high level of achievement? The schools we envision will, as Darling-Hammond put it,

> provide a foundation for a more complex form of teaching practice, one that attends simultaneously to students and their diverse needs on one hand and to the demands of more challenging subject matter standards on the other. (p. 8)

Even more difficult than meeting the demands of "challenging subject matter" is the need to create a generation of highly skilled *learning activists*, students who singly or in groups identify and attack problems and seek new skills as a function of habit and personality. We believe that training such students involves more than recognizing a variety of learning styles or addressing their multiple intelligences. We believe that to produce true learning activists, schools must break down many traditional boundaries, opening to children territory historically reserved for the adults in the building (decision making, planning, assessment) and opening to adults territory historically reserved for the children in the building (productive work in the disciplines). In this way, adults become model lifelong learners engaged with children in a common cause rather than distant, often rather bored guardians of the curriculum.

One way to describe this phenomenon is to say that successful schools will be activist communities rather than static institutions. Activist learning is always productive in the sense that the work teachers and students do together produces more than higher test scores or even clever demonstrations of skill; it has a more "authentic" impact than can be measured by a rubric or contained in a curriculum guide. Activist learning reaches outside the walls of the classroom and reshapes the world. And in the process, the learners—children and adults alike—experience "human excellence, both private and public."

The First Six Essential Elements

The first Essential Element of the Paideia school posits that such a school is student centered, which means that ultimately it nurtures the self-reliance of the individual student by developing his or her own sense of responsibility. If lifelong learning is to be a reality, then it is the job of the teacher to wean the individual student, to create an independent learner who is keenly aware of his or her strengths and weaknesses, in skills as well as knowledge. This self-reliance as a learner does not mean that the individual student forgoes working in a group or does not master the communications skills necessary for teamwork. Rather, it means that the student learns the flexibility required for working effectively with a wide variety of people in a wide variety of configurations. Students carry their inquisitiveness and their skills with them from subject to subject and job to job, relishing the challenges presented first by a demanding education and later by a full and active life. As Merlin tells the Wart (later King Arthur) in T. H. White's *The Once and Future King* (1939), "Education is experience, and the essence of experience is self-reliance" (p. 46). Thus an educational life of rigorous experience—in demanding coached projects and Paideia seminars—prepares every student individually for life in the 21st century, survivable perhaps only when that life is defined by learning.

The Chattanooga School of Arts and Sciences, a K–12 Paideia magnet school in Chattanooga, Tennessee, exemplifies the notion of the school as the incubator of self-reliance. Visitors to the school are always impressed with the powerful seminars they witness, but even more memorable for many are the subtle examples of student maturity and independence. They notice how even elementary students are allowed to use the library independently, as their classwork demands. They are impressed with how young students often approach older students for help and the older students respond generously with their time and attention. They recount how aware even younger students are of their roles and responsibilities in the seminar or in a classroom project. This kind of learning culture has given the Chattanooga School of Arts and Sciences an extremely high rate of graduates going on to community college and university study, much higher than the average for the Chattanooga schools.

The second Essential Element in a Paideia school is student involvement in governance, both individually and as a member of a group. We believe that a classical education equips students for an active public life, preparing them to become the informed, active citizenry that a successful democracy demands. However, neither a course in civics nor a lukewarm student council experience will ready students for life in the 21st century. Rather, we believe students must be taught to internalize discipline and structure such that by the middle school years they have achieved a mature sense of self-discipline or, in other words, a sense of responsibility for their own actions. From the elementary grades on, they should be involved in active student government, both of class and school, such that by the time they reach high school they are capable of being intricately involved in the governance and management of all aspects of the school, including budgetary and personnel decisions.

If this ideal seems impossibly ambitious or naively romantic, consider the example of Federal Hocking High School in Stuart, Ohio. Principal George Wood (author of *Schools That Work*, 1992) and his staff have embraced the challenge of involving students in nearly every aspect of school management and governance. The students have responded enthusiastically, growing into the responsibilities offered them in what Wood terms a "school community rather than an institution." In this way, they have learned by experience what they had previously encountered only in textbooks and civics projects. The lessons formerly relegated to stale academic coursework take on the power and intensity of the "real" world because, of course, the governance of a high school *is* the real world, often involving a nonpersonnel budget of hundreds of thousands of dollars and the lives of dozens of adults and hundreds of students.

The third Essential Element of a Paideia school is that the teachers and administrators model lifelong learning. Any adults who are actively involved in the life of the school should themselves be lifelong learners for several reasons. First, these adults create a critical mass within the culture of the school so that learning is valued in every aspect of school life. Second, each classroom should contain a master craftsman (writer, historian, mathematician, etc.) and a group of apprentices engaged in a common endeavor. This common cause, the active pursuit of a discipline, binds teacher and students together in a collaborative rather than adversarial relationship. In this way, the teacher *models* learning for the student, probably the most profound relationship an adult can adopt toward a child or adolescent. By modeling not just the skills but also the enthusiasm and activism of a true learner, each teacher becomes immediate proof that lifelong learning is an achievable ideal.

Schools, then, should become communities of learners, adults as well as children. In a world that is ever more socially fragmented, community of any sort is becoming increasingly rare. For better or worse, our schools represent the one common experience for our children, and in some instances the burden of raising them has fallen increasingly on teachers and administrators. A Paideia school sees this challenge as an opportunity to build a community in which the members are active participants, trying to understand the world around them and contributing to a better quality of life for all. A Paideia school is held together by a common and fostered love of learning that reaches out to the larger community.

The fourth Essential Element of a Paideia school is that it is the center of a learning community that extends beyond the school. The fifth is that the school cares about the intellectual development of both students and adults. In successful Paideia schools, programs bring in learners from outside the school for knowledge sharing and adult learning programs.

Students have the opportunity to teach, to exhibit, to share their knowledge. The school becomes the focal point for learning in the community. Take, for example, the traditional repository of knowledge in a community, the library, and the traditional gathering place for adult education, the community or recreation center. There are no good educational reasons why the best libraries and community centers should not be in the schools. In this way, adults who model learning come in constant and natural contact with children. Modeling is not only one of the most powerful teaching techniques employed by humans, but it is unavoidable. Children learn the behaviors, beliefs, and habits of their culture by observing and interacting with adults, and some of this takes place during formal schooling.

The students at Community Prep School in Colorado Springs, Colorado, a charter Paideia school for at-risk high school students, take classes in a variety of settings, all of which house businesses or other community organizations. For example, the main campus also serves as headquarters for the local Job Training Partnership Act, a federal program that provides funding for adult education. The proximity of this program creates an environment in which the students are constantly in contact with other learners from the community at large. The students, young and old alike, come and go freely from this main campus as they travel to different classes and to work in local businesses and organizations.

All of the students at Community Prep were labeled severely at-risk in their traditional high schools or had already dropped out of a system that placed them in increasingly restrictive environments both intellectually and physically. At Community Prep they all are developing their intellectual skills and taking responsibility for progressing through the same demanding liberal arts curriculum.

This same sort of reciprocity between community and school is found at Cason Lane Academy in Murfreesboro, Tennessee, a K–8 year-round Paideia school. The brainchild of Superintendent John Hodge Jones, Cason Lane is open from 6:00 a.m. until 7:00 p.m., offering "educational experiences" from 8:00 a.m. until 5:30 p.m. and "extended school services" from 6:00 a.m. to 8:00 a.m. and after school until 7:00 p.m. Extended services are offered 5 days a week, 52 weeks a year; and interim sessions in the year-round calendar offer up to 40 extra days of academic time for enrichment and acceleration. Parents choosing to enroll their students in extended services pay a small fee; however, students directed by school personnel to attend supplementary classes do so at district expense. Mayor Joe Jackson of Murfreesboro argues that "these services support the family by making it possible for people to work without worrying because they know their children are involved in constructive learning." In addition, Cason Lane is now beginning to offer adult education courses to complement the course offerings available to children.

The sixth Essential Element of a Paideia school is that all children are expected to learn and succeed. To a Paideia educator, this is a matter not just of democratic principles but of the very survival of our communities. We therefore reject the current de facto educational caste system in the United States as unjust and undemocratic. It is the worst kept secret in American education that the children of the relatively affluent get well-funded, safe public schools with the best-paid teachers and the highest quality materials while, sometimes only blocks away, the children of others struggle to learn in conditions an underdeveloped country would be ashamed of. Even in the better schools, if children come from non-English-speaking households, are predominately tactile learners, or, perhaps most damning of all, don't have good "test-taking skills," they may be placed from their earliest years in classrooms with low expectations. Too often the result is resentment and substandard education.

Anne Wheelock's 1992 book, *Crossing the Tracks*, summarizes in no uncertain terms the large body of research that proves most forms of tracking do not benefit those labeled gifted or talented, and they have damaging, often disastrous, effects on the "lower" students. For this reason, we believe that in most situations schools must teach most students in heterogeneous groups. Schools like the Pueblo School of Arts and Sciences, a K–12 charter school in Pueblo, Colorado, are designed on this premise and are proving that academic standards need not be lowered in order to teach students more democratically. In fact, compared with tracked schools, untracked schools often raise many more students to the standard and so raise the educational quality of the entire community.

To teach all students successfully, however, we cannot ignore the fact that many arrive at school hungry, cold, or tired. Because a Paideia school emphasizes democratic access to classical education, its natural partner is a business or organization that can help students outside of school. For example, many urban schools now provide a home base for the agencies that serve children and families in need. These programs are aimed at preventing dropouts, rescuing potential failures, and providing a sense of hope and security so that every student may come to the classroom ready to learn, with basic needs met. Such community collaboration not only rallies necessary resources to support children and families, but it also expands the base of financial and human resources needed to create *solutions* for suffering families.

Learning for Life

Ultimately, the classical school as we define it is intended to be an incubator for a life devoted to learning of all kinds. In his whimsical and wise book *The Once and Future King*—itself a vast repository of knowledge—T. H. White (1939) writes:

> The best thing for being sad . . . is to learn something. That is the only thing that never fails. You may grow old and trembling in your anatomies, you may lie awake at night listening to the disorder of your veins, you may miss your only love, you may see the world about you devastated by evil lunatics, or know your honor trampled in the sewers of baser minds. There is only one thing for it then—to learn. Learn why the world wags and what wags it. That is the only thing which the mind can never exhaust, never alienate, never be tortured by, never fear or distrust, and never dream of regretting. Learning is the thing for you. Look at what a lot of things there are to learn—pure science, the only purity there is. You can learn astronomy in a lifetime, natural history in three, literature in six. And then, after you have exhausted a million lifetimes in biology and medicine and theocriticism and geography and history and economics— why, you can start to make a cartwheel out of the appropriate wood, or spend fifty years learning to begin to learn to beat your adversary at fencing. After that you can start again on mathematics, until it is time to learn to plough. (p. 183)

Learning is the ultimate form of power, as long as we remember that it is a verb as well as a noun. We are never defeated as long as we have the power to learn.

A Paideia education gives the lie to two rampant misconceptions about teaching and learning. The first is that high academic standards and near universal student success cannot coexist; schools across the county are proving this is untrue. The second misconception is that teachers and administrators cannot be both caring and rigorous, that somehow the affective and cognitive domains are separate entities. On the contrary, we cannot ask individual students to rise to their potential and expect results if we don't respect and care about them. Nor can we care without expecting the most that they—and we—have to give.

THE PAIDEIA SEMINAR
Terry Roberts

All teachers in a Paideia school use Socratic seminars as a central teaching/ learning device, both schoolwide and integrated into the curriculum.

In many ways, the seminar is the culmination of any unit of study in a Paideia classroom. It is the formal learning event in which students are led to develop and explore their own reaction to a body of information, personalizing learning to a degree that would be otherwise impossible. Furthermore, the seminar is designed to foster a depth of understanding in students that is rare in any school setting, leading to improved ability to think abstractly and problem solve successfully in collaboration with others.

There are strong arguments for using seminar instruction both as an integral part of independent units of study in the classroom and as a schoolwide, shared event. In-class seminars greatly enhance the teaching and learning of various subject areas. At the same time, schoolwide use often leads to more successful staff development in the seminar as a teaching skill and, with thoughtful "text" selection, can help establish a schoolwide theme. All adults who regularly lead seminars with children should themselves participate in regular seminar discussion with peers.

The Classroom Seminar

The seminar is never the exclusive teaching method. Didactic instruction (lecture, demonstration, audiovisual presentation) is the most efficient way to introduce information to students; the coached project is the most powerful way to have them practice the intellectual skills involved in applying that information; and the seminar is the most evocative way to have them investigate the ideas and values inherent to the information.

Classroom seminars can be used for a variety of purposes. For example, the seminar can be an integral part of a character education plan (see Phillip Vincent's *Developing Character in Students*, 1994), in which students are asked to construct a personal response to a human dilemma. The seminar is a valid tool for teaching thinking about math or science, art or music. In a school, district, or state with a clearly defined and rigorous curriculum, it becomes an efficient way to deliver that curriculum because it engages students so thoroughly with the textual material involved. It is a powerful tool for teaching writing across the curriculum and to a variety of students not traditionally successful in the language arts classroom.

The seminar itself is a formal discussion based on a text in which the leader asks only open-ended questions. *Text* in this instance can have widely varied meanings: artwork, music, photographs, video, maps, a math or science problem, and facsimiles of historical documents, as well as more traditional written texts. For a seminar to be effective, however, the group must be able to focus on a common item in order to prevent the formal discussion from disintegrating into a bull session. Within the context of this discussion, students are required to study the text carefully, listen closely to the comments of others, think critically for themselves, and articulate both their own thoughts and their responses to the thoughts of others. From the students' point of view, the seminar differs from most other formal classroom experiences in that it asks them to voice and examine their own thinking at a sophisticated level, not replay the thoughts of teacher or textbook.

To maximize learning for their students, effective seminar leaders are constantly aware of two goals. The first is that all participants be asked to practice traditional communications skills: reading, writing, speaking, listening, and thinking. These skills are the business of all teachers; they empower students in all disciplines and lead them naturally into a life of learning as adults. Students who are fully involved in a successful seminar will have read or heard the text several times and considered it thoroughly before the seminar. The seminar leader will ask them to think about evocative values and ideas throughout—examining, defending, and clarifying their own ideas and those of others. Many seminar leaders also have students write more or less formal statements not only before and after the seminar but also during the seminar itself as a way of enhancing their thinking.

The second goal of seminar leaders is to engage students in higher-order thinking by asking them (and coaching them to ask one another) to summarize, analyze, synthesize, compare, contrast, logically defend, and challenge their own ideas and those of others. A consistent irony in current American education is that we preach constantly about the need to teach students to think without successfully developing a formal process to do so. In the Paideia seminar, students are taught how to express their ideas publicly so that those ideas can be discussed critically. They are asked to think and articulate at a higher level based on a deeper understanding of the subject.

This relationship between seminar experience and student ability to conceptualize and verbalize is now being documented in North Carolina, where end-of-grade writing tests focus on thinking and articulation skills as well as technical ability. These tests are holistically scored, stressing students' ability to clearly organize and justify their thoughts. From 1992 through 1995 students at Githens Middle School in Durham showed dramatic increases in 8th grade writing scores despite decreasing scores from incoming 6th graders and despite the fact that there were no other organized, schoolwide efforts to improve writing. This period of rapid improvement in student writing ability coincided with three years of intense, schoolwide seminar activity. Those who still mistakenly consider Paideia an elitist program should take note that minority students at Githens showed the greatest gains in writing ability. Similar gains occurred over a much larger sample of schools from 1994 through 1996 in Guilford County, North Carolina, where students in the 12 elementary schools that had implemented the seminar showed consistent increases in 4th grade writing scores.

To teach higher-order thinking and articulation skills, teachers need to use texts that are rich in ideas, introducing students early on to seminar discussion of classical literature, historical documents, and other primary source materials. For example, in a unit on the Battle of Gettysburg, an obvious "classical" text is the "Gettysburg Address." Although in the interest of cultural literacy students should read Lincoln's speech closely, it is not the only appropriate text associated with the battle. Other primary historical documents like soldiers' letters; contemporary newspaper accounts (which should be examined for accuracy); writing by African Americans; and the journals, diaries, or letters of women whose loved ones were involved in the fighting can make excellent seminar readings because they personalize the internal as well as external conflicts. These texts may not have had the historical impact of Lincoln's brief speech, but many of them are powerful and thought provoking.

Although Adler's original reading lists (see *The Paideia Program*, 1984) are somewhat narrow in their emphasis on certain elements of European cultural history, they still serve as a dependable starting point in identifying powerful seminar texts from Western culture before 1950. Teachers and administrators who wish to engage students with exciting and relevant texts should remember that a classic—contemporary or ancient—is a classic primarily because it speaks powerfully to a wide variety of people over a significant period of time. Classics are by definition always relevant and almost always exciting if teachers can help students understand them properly. For many students and teachers, the seminar process is perhaps the most inviting doorway into works they might otherwise never read.

Teachers should be constantly on the lookout for any text that will engage students in the learning process, keeping in mind that "classics" are often discovered or rediscovered years after their creation. In expanding their lists of powerful seminar texts, teachers can use this general checklist of qualities. A good seminar text

- Is thought provoking; it is not easy to dispose of intellectually;
- Concerns ideas and values of some complexity;
- Is evocative and, in some sense, open-ended; there is more to discussing it than either agreeing or disagreeing with its theme;
- Concerns a number of essential issues and so elicits a variety of responses from a variety of people;
- Deals with issues of some particular concern for the intended participants; and

• Fits coherently into the curriculum of the school or classroom where it is used.

Teachers also need to ask themselves whether or not they are consistently asking students to examine and talk about works they might not discuss otherwise—for example, nonwritten texts like art, photographs, maps, and musical compositions.

In its most recent seminar lists, the National Paideia Center has folded Adler's original "great books" list into a number of reading lists developed by teachers and parents in schools throughout the United States that include grade-level-appropriate works by women and cultural minorities. In addition, the center's list has sections devoted to math, science, and social studies that include not only appropriate texts but also reference books and Internet sites that are excellent resources.

To introduce seminar teaching, Adler originally recommended a technique he called the "Wednesday Revolution," a schoolwide seminar period built into the schedule once a week. A number of schools around the United States have adopted this idea as a first step in implementing the Paideia philosophy. It allows administrators and teachers to ensure that all faculty members are actually leading seminars. Unfortunately, many schools stop there. Neither teachers nor students come to see the full value of seminars, and the seminars themselves seldom become more than exercises in discussion skills. Again, the goal should be to use the seminar as a natural part of a unit of study, and the school goal should be to integrate seminars into the life of every classroom in the building.

The Seminar's Larger Role

Administrators and teachers designing a Paideia school should plan from the beginning to integrate seminars into the natural intellectual growth of the total school community as well as into individual classrooms within the school. There are a number of ways to integrate the seminar into the life of the total school community. Formal seminar discussion of documents that inform a school's improvement plan should be an integral experience for parents and faculty. For example, a school community that is making the transition from a traditional junior high to a student-centered middle school can conduct a series of seminars on middle school philosophy and implementation as well as team teaching and planning concepts, flexible scheduling, and adolescent psychology. It is vital that these discussions be a regular part of every teacher's life and that parents be encouraged to attend regularly.

This sort of formal, professional questioning, however, is not enough to enhance the true intellectual development of the adult school community. Teachers, administrators, and other adults concerned with the school need to be part of an ongoing seminar series designed to sharpen their own appreciation of historical documents, works of literature, issues on mathematics and science, drama, and the visual arts. Such events have a number of essential results:

1. Children see adults modeling lifelong learning.

2. Interested adults come to understand the seminar program in the school from the best perspective of all—the seminar itself.

3. A significant number of community residents become involved in school seminars, often as volunteer or substitute seminar leaders.

4. Communitywide seminar involvement can sustain a Paideia program in a school during transitions in administration and turnover in faculty.

True seminar discussion and a wide base of support require that educators recruit participants from a cross-section of the community (in terms of race, income, and so forth). Offering on-site child care and van or bus transportation will encourage participation in evening seminars.

Teachers throughout the United States use the schoolwide seminar in powerful ways. In elementary schools, teachers often work in grade-level teams to choose texts and write questions, providing support to individual teachers and creating a strong inducement for common planning and instructional alignment. In middle schools, vertical or horizontal teams often choose seminar texts and write questions together as a way of truly integrating both instruction and curriculum across subject areas. And in high schools, teachers working in vertical houses or in horizontal teams choose texts and write questions together to provide their students with a common learning event in a school day that is otherwise fragmented and unfocused.

Seminars in the Elementary School

During the mid- to late-1980s some people questioned whether teachers should even attempt seminars with students in primary grades; Adler himself offered contradictory statements on this question. What has become clear during recent years, however, is that seminar discussion is a reasonable teaching strategy even in kindergarten, and that it enhances elementary teachers' ability to teach young children sophisticated thinking and articulation skills.

At Madison Elementary School in Guilford County, North Carolina, teachers have evolved in their use of the seminar, fully integrating it into coached units of study (see Chapter 3). Teachers at Madison plan together at grade level, and they use seminars to enhance carefully constructed units in which each day's instruction has been charted using the three-column template. In their 2nd grade classrooms, for example, teachers Diane Odroneic, Beverly Lee, Bruce Curtis, and Brenda McGee integrate at least one seminar into their unit on Communities and Democracies. They use one of the following texts, depending on the makeup of a given class or on individual goals: *Heron Street* by Ann Turner, *Abiyoyo* by Pete Seeger, *Ox-Cart Man* by Donald Hall, *Sanji and the Baker* by Robin Tzannes and Korky Paul, and *A Chair for My Mother* by Vera B. Williams. Lee and Odroneic explain that

> *Heron Street* deals with ecosystems, and we use it to discuss both positive and negative changes that can occur within a system or community. *Sanji and the Baker*, on the other hand, deals directly with the role of the justice system. We vary the seminar text in response to student interests and the curriculum goals we need to cover, but we're always careful to use a text that complements the didactic instruction and coaching that we have done as part of a project.

Among elementary schools currently using seminar instruction, Brentmoor Elementary in Mentor, Ohio, has created an exemplary community seminar program, showcasing for parents at night the same process that students participate in during the day. One snowy evening in February 1996, I visited Brentmoor on community seminar night. The media center was decorated to reflect the evening's text, a scene from *Phantom of the Opera*. Even the name tags and napkins bore the emblem of the Phantom's mask. When the parents arrived, they sat down in the seminar circle and were given the dialogue from the scene they were about to hear. Before reading the "text," however, they listened to a recording of the scene. As they listened, they were supposed to sketch a continuous line drawing that reflected the music. Parents participated enthusiastically, sharing their drawings and the meaning they derived from the scene. The seminar continued with a detailed discussion of the dialogue sung in the scene. When the seminar finally broke up, parents continued to discuss the music and the language as they shared refreshments and eventually left the building.

Two teachers and a parent planned this seminar, and a group of teachers and parents provided decorations, art supplies, and refreshments. As principal George Jaroscak explains,

> Once a parent has participated in one of our community seminars, we have a natural ally for the seminar process with students. Not only that, but system administrators and teachers from other buildings who have questions about the seminar can be introduced to the process in the most natural way possible—by participating in one.

Although attendance varies at Brentmoor's community seminars, Jaroscak and his supporters continue to offer as sophisticated an experience as possible, intending not only to build public support for the Paideia program but also to enhance their own learning and that of any adult who participates.

Seminars in the Middle School

The natural role of the seminar in a middle school is to unite teams of teachers and students around a common learning event and to help those same teams plan and present a truly integrated curriculum. After planning collaboratively, the teachers use common texts and sets of questions to address thematically linked units of study that cut across all the core subject areas.

To reach this ultimate organizational goal, many middle schools begin with a schoolwide, biweekly seminar program designed to prepare the teachers as discussion leaders and to teach the students to respond to demanding textual material. From there, they expand their use of the technique to include seminars planned and implemented teamwide, using texts that integrate the subject areas represented on the team. For example, Githens Middle School teachers in Durham, North Carolina, created an 8th grade unit on justice, which included seminars on *The Man Without a Country, Inherit the Wind* (which deals with the Scopes trial), "Letter from Birmingham Jail," and the "Virginia Stamp Act Resolutions." Because every student on the team had these seminar discussions in common and because teachers were free to use texts from all subject areas, these seminars integrated the unit on justice for every student.

Seminars in the High School

Constructive use of the seminar in high schools has been hampered by two traditional structures: the hour-long instructional block and division of the curriculum into discrete subjects. Although some innovative schools like the Chattanooga School of Arts and Sciences and the newer Pueblo School of Arts and Sciences (both K–12 public magnet programs) have investigated ways to integrate subject area instruction, the traditional high school has proven the most difficult arena for use of the seminar.

Fortunately, recent scheduling reforms have created longer instructional blocks in many schools, making the seminar logistically possible (see Chapter 6). A number of high schools are now exploring the Paideia philosophy and using seminars to teach conceptual thinking across the disciplines.

Measuring Success

A school that uses seminars extensively can measure its success by asking these questions:

• Have both teachers and students come to value intellectual exchange? Are they engaging more naturally in discussion of ideas, principles, and values both in and out of class?

- Are more books (not textbooks), historical documents, works of art, musical compositions, and dramatic productions being read, watched, and listened to closely? Are they being widely discussed?
- Are both teachers and students thinking more critically, resolving more conflicts with respectful discussion rather than argument, and listening more carefully to one another?
- Has attendance of both teachers and students improved? Does the climate of the seminar nurture the learning of both?
- Do more and more—eventually all—students and teachers feel they have an important voice in the school?
- Are seminars being used regularly in every classroom in the building?
- Are teachers and administrators regularly involved in faculty seminars? Are community seminars a regular part of the learning life of the school community?
- Are the faculty and administrators working hard to improve the quality of the seminars?

Students should become so used to the seminar process that they automatically assume they will have at least one formal seminar as a part of every unit of study. In well-taught classrooms, students look forward to seminars because, whether they verbalize it or not, all children want a world rich in learning and a voice with which to engage that world.

INTELLECTUAL COACHING

Lois Johnson

All teachers in a Paideia school use coaching for the majority of their instructional program.

Intellectual coaching accounts for 60 to 80 percent of instructional time in a Paideia classroom, yet it has proven to be the hardest of the three Paideia columns to define. Mortimer Adler and Ted Sizer originally described coaching as if it could occur only in a tutorial or small-group situation (see Adler, 1984, Chapter 2). This restriction complicated implementation for the average public school teacher, whose class size may be as large as 35. Also, the original description did not formalize coaching as a teaching technique in the way that the seminar was formalized. This lack of clarity led to some doubt and disagreement about whether coaching was actually very different from the types of guided practice or cooperative learning commonly used in many U.S. schools. As defined here, intellectual coaching draws on the original definition of Adler and Sizer but takes the concept to a more formal stage, permitting teachers to be trained, critically observed, and eventually attain mastery as coaches.

This new, clearer description of intellectual coaching establishes the teacher-student relationship within a formal, real-world, product-oriented classroom project. It should be noted here that the coached classroom project owes as much to the classroom practice of Foxfire, expeditionary learning, and cooperative learning as it does to Adler and Sizer's definition. In other words, it draws on a number of complementary trends to create a second column with as dramatic an impact on the learning lives of students as the Paideia seminar. Because coaching occupies so much instructional time in a Paideia classroom, the product-oriented project often becomes the organizing principle for all three columns.

Coaching consists of the various kinds of facilitation of student work that occur when students participate in projects singly or in groups and are coached by their teachers, by one another, and by outside experts. The defining characteristic of these academic projects is their culmination in a product of real-world value, thus motivating students to practice intently the skills involved in producing the product.

Ideally, the project that teachers are asking students to produce is a quality product that involves several academic disciplines and most or all of Gardner's seven intelligences (see Gardner, 1983). Thus, students can illustrate their strengths according to their particular learning styles. The project can be as short as a class period or as long as a school year. The product itself can be as short as a haiku embedded in a drawing or as long as a dramatic production, a student-built structure, or a book.

As always in the Paideia classroom, students are coached in heterogeneous groups, and each group is held accountable by themselves and the coach for the quality of their product. Accountability is performance-based and noncompetitive, and within this framework, individual student achievement is evaluated according to individual progress rather than standardized measures. (Portfolios combined with narrative evaluations are a natural complement to the coaching process.)

The most instructive way to think about the quality of the coaching process is not in terms of what the *teacher does*, but rather in terms of what the *students experience*. That is why the 12 Principles of Intellectual Coaching are written specifically from the student's point of view (see fig. 3.1).

Roles and Setting

In an active Paideia classroom, not only will the roles of the teacher and the students vary substantially from those in the traditional classroom, but the physical setting of the classroom must change as well. The teacher as coach is like the master craftsman at work in a shop, surrounded by

FIGURE 3.1
The 12 Principles of Intellectual Coaching

1. Students discover and construct their own meaning out of the project in a personally significant way. (For example, they may help design the assignment as well as the ways in which they will be evaluated.)

2. Students exercise their own power of choice in an increasingly responsible and mature way.

3. Students build on the past and anticipate the future, their own and that of others.

4. The individual student defines himself or herself through the process, both interpersonally and intrapersonally.

5. The individual student validates his or her sense of control and competence as his or her expectations of success are confirmed and challenged.

6. The various tasks that are part of the process are relevant to the individual students and have obvious value in the world outside the classroom.

7. The tasks involved in the process are both challenging and novel.

8. Students are not motivated by negative cognitions or emotions—including almost all those associated with traditional, competitive grades.

9. Students successfully communicate and cooperate with a wide variety of others in a wide variety of settings.

10. Individual students treat one another with respect and courtesy, stressing that each has unique and valuable talents.

11. Cultural and environmental differences among individual students and among those others associated with the project are not only accepted, but they are valued.

12. Students periodically review the process and evaluate how and what they are learning (and not learning).

apprentices. The teacher, a recognized expert in the process at hand, is actively involved with the apprentices in creating the product. In this role, the teacher helps students perfect their skills so that the end product of their common labor is of the highest quality.

By the same token, students can be compared to apprentices. They work closely with the teacher, either alone or with other students, learning by doing all the various tasks involved in producing the product. The skill level of the apprentice (student) may vary from novice to near master; the defining element of effective learning is that every student is constantly improving. Just as no apprentice can gain mastery by learning only a few of the many jobs involved in producing the shop's best work, so the student must learn a large number of interrelated tasks to assure the quality of the work.

Perhaps these changing roles of teacher and student can best be illustrated in the following example. A group of 11th grade language arts students in a course on American literature are exploring 20th century American culture and ideas. They stage a production of *Inherit the Wind,* a 1955 drama based on the infamous Scopes "monkey trial" in Tennessee in which a young science teacher was tried and convicted of teaching evolution. The language arts teacher directs the play, the preparations (including a seminar on the text) and rehearsals make up the coached "process," and the production itself is the product. The teacher, like any drama director, will take on many roles during the time between the first read-through and closing night, but ultimately the teacher's job is to bring out the best work possible from every student involved in each aspect of the production.

Every student in that 11th grade class will play a key role in creating the highest quality production possible, including those involved in set design and construction, costuming, makeup, and script editing, as well as those who actually perform the various roles. Students find it necessary to stay focused while working alone, and they have to work closely with groups of other students and adults as well. The necessary intellectual skills specific to language arts alone include reading, writing, speaking, listening, thinking—the entire gamut of literacy. Most important, the quality of the production itself gives the work meaning for the students. When teachers of different subject areas can collaborate on the project, it becomes an even richer experience for the students as they begin to understand the relationships that link subjects together.

Obviously, the activities described above will require altering the traditional classroom setting of desks in neat lines facing the teacher's desk in the front of the room. In fact, no one setting is right for all activities—the room setting will be determined by the work in production. To get a good idea of what this might mean, visit a local high school and examine the following rooms: any traditional shop or vocational classroom—carpentry, masonry, agriculture, mechanics, nursing, where students are learning skills specific to a trade; the drama, choral, or instrumental music room, where students are preparing for a performance; the yearbook or journalism staff room, where students are preparing this year's annual or the next issue of the school paper; the art room where students are preparing an exhibition of student work.

The common factors that unite these spaces are the involvement of students in active learning by doing and the sense of quality control imposed by having to produce a product of real worth. In much the same way, academic coaching requires that the classroom be organized according to the project currently under way: play rehearsal, book production, historical simulation, math textbook composition, or science experiments.

Looking into the Paideia classroom may be startling because it is sometimes *empty*. Just as vocational teachers take students off campus to "live project" sites where they build homes, repair school property, or perform community service projects, teachers who become expert intellectual coaches also discover that their individual classrooms must be fluid in design. Sometimes they even find it necessary to go beyond the classroom itself to obtain the highest quality work. The Paideia teacher and student will find that Adler was correct when he said that the world is a classroom for the lifelong learner and that all learning is not confined within four walls.

Of the three Paideia columns, coaching is the teaching and learning construct that breaks down most of the traditional school barriers that *limit* learning. Coaching requires some flexibility in terms of time (longer units of time for focused student labor), space (taking student to "live" settings for academic projects), materials (the raw material of production), the role of the teacher (use of outside experts and peer coaching), and the role of the student (planner, designer, worker, quality control engineer).

If the first Paideia column, *didactic instruction*, is designed to relay factual knowledge, then the second column, *intellectual coaching*, is designed to allow students to manipulate and apply that knowledge. In doing so, they master not only the knowledge base itself but also the skillful self-reliance that leads directly to lifelong learning.

Although some academic teachers are disdainful of athletic coaches, those same teachers are often surprised that there is much to be learned from the techniques of those coaches. The best coach certainly spends time acquainting students (the team) with the fundamentals of the sport—but then sends the students out to practice those fundamentals, under coaching guidance. This process allows the coach to determine the skill of each student in applying the fundamentals of the sport and permits a lot of one-on-one supervision and guidance, culminating in performance in the "big game." By reviewing the players' performance in that culminating activity, again the coach has an opportunity to identify weaknesses and pinpoint areas to reteach or revise in the best interests of the team and the individual players.

The Paideia program suggests that didactic instruction should rarely exceed 10 percent of instructional time; and even then the discussion should intellectually challenge students. In place of extended lecture, Paideia Center staff recommends that coaching activities make up at least 65 percent of instructional time. Such activities may vary from individual writing to large projects or productions that involve months of research or other effort. By teaching students how to manipulate and apply the information under consideration, coaching activities aim to teach them to master the intellectual skills involved.

Exemplary Coaching

The Darnell-Cookman Middle School in Jacksonville, Florida, exemplifies excellent coaching activities. Formerly an inner-city neighborhood school, it opened in August 1993 as a complete Paideia school designated as a magnet for gifted and talented students. Because the school has no entrance requirements, Darnell-Cookman students have as broad a range of abilities as students in any neighborhood school. Students who score from 0 percent to 100 percent on standardized tests are heterogeneously grouped for all instruction. Faculty members range from novices to veterans of up to 30 years. Some stayed with the school through its program change; others came from all over the system because they were intrigued by the possibilities of the Paideia program and the opportunity it provided for their own professional growth.

Training for the faculty was offered during two weeks in the summer before the school opened. One week was devoted to intensive training on using the seminar as a schoolwide activity and as a tool in the individual classroom. The second week focused on coaching techniques as an alternative to the lectures, worksheets, textbooks, and audiovisuals that have permeated the traditional classroom. The most difficult step, it became immediately evident, was the first one—teachers needed to mentally relinquish their position as the focal point of the classroom to allow students to take center stage for most of the instructional time. Initially teachers admitted being distrustful and unsure whether students were "getting it," and many reverted to lecture format. But as student participation and interest grew dramatically, the teachers realized that lecture really was not necessary.

Ron Hafner, a 6th grade team leader and language arts teacher, told me he first realized the impact of Paideia on his students one day in October during the first year. He had been called to the office at the end of a period for an emergency phone call. As is often the case, the call ran over to the next period. Afterward, Ron rushed down the hall, expecting to find chaos in his classroom. At first, he was amazed to find that he was not hearing disruptive noises. Then, he was astounded to find his students already in their coaching groups and involved in the activities they had begun the previous day.

Teachers on Henry Colado's 8th grade team were especially adept at involving their whole team (including more than 140 students) in the many coaching activities they had designed as part of a unit on the role of minorities and the impact of the telegraph during the Civil War. Henry teaches history; Elaine Ussery, math; Charlie Tanner, science; and Jenny Sorrells, language arts. The middle school configuration gave them four consecutive periods to use as needed for all the coaching projects and field trips, and for whole-team assemblies consisting of presentations by speakers and performing groups from the community.

One day when I was visiting, four groups of students (one group from each classroom) were in the courtyard preparing to construct a campsite that would accurately illustrate how the military lived at the site of the Battle of Olustee. Wood, stones, tools, and other items were scattered everywhere, and 20 kids were discussing what tasks were necessary and how they should be done. Although the courtyard was a busy place, it was obvious that all activity was on task. Almost immediately members of the group assigned to construct the shelter disagreed on how to go about the task. After each student expressed a reason for his or her point of view, I was surprised to hear the group suggest that they try two of the most promising suggestions on a small scale to see which would be the most effective method of construction. After trying both, the group agreed that one design was superior.

Meanwhile, four other teams of students were in the science teacher's classroom, drawing schematics for a working telegraph, which they would install in and around the building and link to the campsite being constructed in the courtyard. It was obvious from their frequent references that the group had researched the major features of a working telegraph, as well as the telegraph's influence on the Battle of Olustee. Comments such as "Remember what it said about the junctures needing to be reinforced" indicated that students were citing practical information they had gleaned from previous learning.

In the math classroom, groups of students were working on the logistics for "viewing day." They needed to figure out how to move all the students who were not on their team through the campsite area. They would need enough time for classmates to explain the workings of the campsite and the telegraph and to give every student a taste of "sojer stew," a delicacy that was to be cooked over a campfire at the site. In addition, the groups were planning short, whole-school assemblies, including a performance by the Sea Island Singers, who would entertain the students with relevant songs and information.

In the language arts classroom, four groups of students were planning the costumes students would wear at the campsite. They too had thoroughly researched the clothing of the 1860s and frequently referred to their sources (books about costuming and vintage clothing gleaned from local college libraries and community drama groups) in discussions of how to make their costumes authentic. Clothing without zippers, fabric without manmade materials, and "strange" styles obviously challenged their imagination and creativity.

None of these areas were quiet enclaves, nor were students sitting in rows with eyes and ears riveted to the teacher. What was obvious at every activity site was the students' intense involvement in the process and their understanding that part of their responsibility was actually teaching others about the particular segment of the project they had been assigned.

The teachers at Darnell-Cookman Middle School are well on their way to providing their students with the classical education of the 21st century. The school is benefiting because they have made a whole-school transition, with almost all teachers using high-quality intellectual coaching techniques combined with interactive didactic instruction and the Paideia seminar. After the first two years, the 7th and 8th grade teachers were delighted to see students entering their classes already trained as 6th graders to participate in coached projects and seminars. With such capable students, teachers can expand the depth and quantity of material they explore.

Nourishing the Spirit of Inquiry

Together, intellectual coaching and the Socratic seminar provide a way to combine the classical education that Robert Hutchins and E. D. Hirsch recommend with Dewey's progressive ideas about learning. Classical education for the 21st century will differ from earlier versions in some significant ways. Although it will retain the richness of in-depth study of human experience and thought, it will also feature student-centered classrooms in which students are actively engaged in design, research, and creation of products with personal value and relevance. Students will have the opportunity to choose topics, activities, and roles of special interest to them.

These coaching activities are especially valuable because they permit all students to demonstrate their strengths. In addition, they encourage students to exert maximum effort, working always toward a rigorous standard. The students, in effect, set their own goals and challenges beyond those set by the teacher. Much of the boredom that students complain about in traditional classrooms stems from teachers having such low expectations that the work they assign is almost an insult to students who know they are capable of more. In the coached classroom, no artificial boundary stops students from going to greater depth.

Coaching gives the student the opportunity to use the information and ideas that are presented didactically and, in the process, hone the skills that will be the foundation of further learning. Through coaching, students learn how to work with others effectively, to value team effort, and to understand their responsibility to the community. In other words, they can work consciously at becoming a fully realized human being. The classical education of the 21st century will nourish the spirit of inquiry that is the hallmark of Western civilization—our common heritage and common right.

DIDACTIC INSTRUCTION
William Chesser

All of the teachers in a Paideia school use relatively little didactic teaching, and that which they use is of a very high quality.

From the beginnings of contemporary school reform, educators have lamented the limitations and overuse of didactic instruction. We deplore its passivity, its inability to impart skills or durable information, and its inappropriateness for certain students and certain subject matter. Yet it continues to dominate classrooms in the United States. This phenomenon puzzles and frustrates administrators, reformers, and teachers like few other issues in modern schooling. If this problem is so obvious, why have we been unable to correct it?

One reason is that although didactic teaching is dreadfully overused, it is nonetheless essential—for example, for introducing and organizing new information in a unit of study. All didactic instruction, however, is not created equal, and it is not enough to merely decry its overuse. Although it is important to remind ourselves continually of the need to limit didactic instruction, we must also move on to the more complex task of clearly outlining the features and characteristics that separate high-quality didactic instruction from mediocre.

Traditionally, didactic instruction has comprised five classroom activities: lecture, reading for content, use of audiovisuals, performance, and demonstration. The list may be expanded to include the use of technology, namely the Internet for information retrieval, but some may argue that this is simply a form of reading for content. What is important is what these exercises have in common: each is a method for delivering information essential to a unit of study.

Many teachers, understanding intuitively that lecture is the most efficient means of distributing information, stick to it almost exclusively in the name of covering content. The problem, of course, is that this is not good teaching. Access to information does not equal learning. In fact, research suggests that few students remember for any significant period more than 5 or 10 percent of the information they receive in lectures. Although lecture is often the most efficient way to *deliver* information, it is rarely the most efficient way to *impart* it, and even though the teacher may cover a great deal of material in a lecture-dominated class, the method practically assures low rates of retention.

Part of the reason why lecture inspires such poor retention is that it places the student in such a passive position. In 1956 educational psychologist Benjamin Bloom outlined a Taxonomy of Thinking Skills, comprising knowledge, comprehension, application, analysis, synthesis, and evaluation. Of the skills in Bloom's taxonomy, lecture can deal with only the simplest: knowledge-level thinking. The student cannot interpret, analyze, or apply new information, much less acquire and hone skills, in a lecture because those exercises require active involvement by the student. By its very design didactic instruction allows that only one person in the room be more than marginally active: the teacher. Students who sit quietly, listening and jotting notes, are not asked to use, and therefore will not develop, thinking skills beyond simple recall.

Adler has spoken of a lecture as the transfer of information from the notes of the presenter to the notes of the audience without passing through the brain of either. Well-trained didactic presenters focus their efforts on making sure the information they present passes through the minds of the students on the way to being recorded in their notes. This often means using a wide variety of didactic techniques within the same presentation. It also means that most effective didactic lessons are short, dramatic, and dense with vital information. An effective didactic lesson has three key elements:

• Organization (handouts, overheads, outlines, advanced organizers, mind maps);

• Energy (enthusiasm, task variation, command of content, penetrating questioning); and

• Boundaries (those things that help ensure bounded content and bounded time).

Organization

Identifying the "must know" core of information from the lesson plan and organizing it clearly is the first step in preparing a didactic lesson. Then the teacher may design high-quality organizer materials—both handouts and audiovisuals—to reflect that organization. The presenter should carefully plan how the students will be led to interact both with the material and the presenter, pacing those interactions carefully throughout the lesson. Handouts should include ample space for note taking. A common mistake of novice lecturers is crowding lesson outlines with so much information that the outlines become confusing or frustrating. Most of the space on a lecture handout should be blank space in which the student can write.

Typically, a good didactic teacher outlines the material to be presented in a handout or on the chalkboard before the lesson. Students can thereby anticipate both where the presentation is going and how the presenter intends to take them there. Before beginning the lesson, the presenter should briefly go over this outline, stressing what the students should know or be able to do after the presentation is over (even if it is very short). This quick overview gives the students a target against which they can judge their own learning (or ignorance) at the end of the lesson. Many quality systems currently available can help students learn how to outline and map information. To the extent these instruments help to develop a logical structure in lessons, they are highly recommended. It is a mistake, however, to rely on such materials to help students infer organization from a presentation.

A final organizational concern is the physical layout of the workspace. The traditional classroom arrangement of student chairs in straight rows facing the front of the room and the teacher's desk as podium is a bad arrangement for a didactic presentation. Straight rows block the direct lines of sight and hearing that are crucial for good didactic teaching, and they banish certain students to the back of the classroom, far from the action.

When arranging a classroom for lecture, audiovisual presentation, or demonstration, a wise educator takes the lead from those institutions that are most successful in didactic presentations: the best-designed churches, theaters, and stadiums.

A good rule is to take the maximum number of students expected and arrange their seats so that they can all be placed as close to the presentation point as possible while maintaining clear sight lines and freedom of movement for the presenter. At times a lab table or a piece of audiovisual equipment will dictate classroom arrangement, but when the presenter is the only point of interest, a good arrangement is a slightly open circle or semicircle that brings students closer to the teacher. If this is not possible, the teacher can move about during the lecture.

Energy

Quality presenters use techniques designed specifically to enhance the overall energy of the session, making the experience as intellectually active as possible for the audience. No matter how organized and informed a presenter is, if he or she cannot stir the minds of the audience, the learning will not be powerful.

Good presenters typically share certain characteristics that energize the audience. First, they are enthusiastic, both about their audience and the material under discussion. Second, they are dynamic, often moving around the room while they speak and involving the audience by asking and answering questions to highlight key points. Like actors assuming roles, they use the full resources of their voices and body language to engage and hold the audience's attention. This kind of strong lecturing is not an issue of personality or personal style. Even people with rather timid personalities can acquire the skills of captivating the audience. Jeannie Boyd, for example, is a Paideia high school teacher in Washington, North Carolina, who does not consider herself an especially outgoing, forceful person. She has learned, however, to "turn on the juice" during didactic presentations to achieve the level of audience engagement she needs.

Another good energizer is variety. Although the primary didactic teaching tool is the lecture, good presenters prepare a variety of other didactic techniques (reading materials, handouts, audiovisuals, overhead projections, video or computer projections, demonstrations, or performance elements) to use together or in sequence. Several of these elements can enhance any basic lecture presentation, particularly by encouraging active discussion among students and presenter.

Discussion, incidentally, is the natural outgrowth of any strong didactic presentation, and it should be encouraged up to a point. The teacher never wants to miss the pursuit of a genuinely teachable moment; however, when discussion distracts students from the topic at hand or lengthens the lesson to the point where students begin to lose interest, an effective teacher postpones discussion and returns to the lecture.

Finally, perhaps the simplest way for a presenter to energize didactic instruction is to move. Movement stimulates the audience by requiring more active attention, and few things can focus a student's flagging concentration like the immediate proximity of the teacher. Mastering the information will free the presenter from the need to be tied to a set of notes at a podium or desk. Although direct quotes from original sources or key historical figures can be powerful in a lecture, even they should be kept short and used sparingly. The presenter should be able to move freely around the room so that he or she can stand beside a sleepy or disruptive student or group while continuing to lecture or to conduct direct discussion. From a student's point of view there is a dramatic difference in listening to a lecture from a stationary speaker as opposed to a mobile presenter who is demonstrating, questioning, explaining, and illustrating.

Boundaries

Boundaries ensure that didactic lessons are short and direct. In a Paideia classroom "effective presentation" means more than brief; it also means students are at the highest possible level of engagement with both material and presenter, so they comprehend and digest the information at hand. Instruments that help teachers identify and keep to rigid, logical boundaries of time and material are therefore essential for achieving the highest-quality didactic presentation.

After identifying a small, logically bounded area of information to be covered in a single session, a presenter should be able to write a simple, one-sentence description of the purpose of the lesson. If this is impossible, the presenter may be trying to accomplish too much and should consider paring down the content. It also helps to give each component of the presentation a specific time allotment and to make every effort to stay on schedule. Many presenters recruit a timekeeper in the audience (if high-quality advanced organizers have been distributed, this assignment should be little if any extra burden for an audience member). Audience involvement is also usually a powerful incentive to stay on schedule.

If the goal of a didactic session is to convey a coherent body of factual knowledge as efficiently as possible, the use of visual and aural aids, handouts, demonstrations, and discussion should *intensify* a didactic lesson, not lengthen or diffuse it. For example, one videotaped scene from *Hamlet* illuminates a discussion of blank verse, whereas seeing the entire play buries it. A short discussion of the pattern of prime numbers may peak student interest, but a belabored treatment of the subject will most often kill it. A handout that outlines the information in a lecture through a series of questions guides the students in their note taking without giving away all the information. Ultimately, whatever clouds or digresses from the main purpose of the lecture can almost always be omitted.

What is most important to remember is this: The best didactic lessons are short and occasional. They are to the point, and teachers must plan the use of instructional materials to sharpen that point.

Didactic instruction presents a twofold problem. First, because didactic teaching is by nature about information, it never gets beyond the lowest levels of thinking skills (namely memorization and recitation). A classroom dominated by lecture is therefore a classroom where children's thinking skills are not properly challenged and honed. Second, contrary to its traditional treatment by schools of education, didactic instruction is not a one-dimensional, natural skill. Good didactic instruction requires teachers to have a large set of sophisticated skills gained only through training and experience.

THE PAIDEIA CURRICULUM

Michael Hale

A Paideia school stresses the same integrated core curriculum for all the students and teaches all the students in heterogeneous groups.

In the first chapter of *The Paideia Proposal*, entitled "Democracy and Education," Mortimer Adler (1982) argues that we have failed to meet the challenge that John Dewey set before us in his book of the same title. Adler notes that the universal suffrage and universal schooling that have become the right of all U.S. citizens are inextricably linked: "The one without the other is a perilous delusion. Suffrage without schooling produces mobocracy, not democracy—not rule of law, not constitutional government by the people as well as for them" (p. 3). We have failed because we have achieved only the same quantity of public schooling, not the same quality. *The remedy for this inequity is a rigorous, meaningful, and integrated core curriculum for all students.*

A challenging intellectual curriculum lies at the heart of Paideia philosophy because we have not yet achieved the *equality* of educational opportunity for all children that is a necessary element of participatory government. Equality of educational opportunity, states Adler (1982), is not provided

> if it means no more than taking the children into the public schools for the same number of hours, days, and years. If once there they are divided into the sheep and the goats, into those destined solely for toil and those destined for economic and political leadership and for a quality of life to which all should have access, then the democratic purpose has been undermined by an inadequate system of public schooling. (p. 5)

The goal of equal educational opportunity thus requires not only equality among schools but also within them. That is, schooling must include a curriculum that enables *all* children to actively engage with and develop a solid foundation of knowledge and skills, delivered by means of a single-track system. This foundation involves meaningful intellectual engagement with subject matter that includes mathematics, language arts, social studies, science, physical education, fine arts (including music), and foreign language. Students' interactions with all of these subjects should be successively more complex and difficult from the 1st through the 12th grade (Adler, 1982, p. 22).

The Paideia curriculum is integrated in the sense that disciplines are considered and taught as part of the whole of human experience, not as distinct entities. To do this, Paideia educators organize curriculum around themes that connect various subject matters and, when possible, link them through the creation of a coached product (see Chapter 3). For example, students studying the French Revolution while developing the theme of change might understand the guillotine as a product of technological changes in a particular historical context, as well as understand the changes that resulted from its political use. Students may apply algebra and geometry in building a miniature guillotine; conduct experiments to determine cutting power; engage in a seminar on a first-person account of the death of Louis XVI written by Henry Essex Edgeworth de Firmont, his personal priest;[1] and write articles from the perspective of a journalist witnessing the event for publication in the period newspaper the class develops as a coached project. This integration is important because the world beyond schooling is integrated, and to lead a full life requires the ability to make and transfer connections.

Engaging all children in this type of curriculum means the end of tracking students into higher and lower courses of study. This does not simply mean that all students should be in what we currently call the higher track. The single track of an integrated core curriculum in a Paideia school is a fundamentally different approach to schooling than what takes place

---

[1]This account is included in a collection of primary historical documents entitled *Eyewitness to History*, edited by John Carey (1987).

in most schools today; it is designed to prepare students for the three callings of adult life laid out by the Paideia Group.

The Curriculum and the Three Callings

The first calling is to earn a decent livelihood, and becoming an activist learner, as described in Chapter 1, is the key to employability now and increasingly in the future. As A. Graham Down (1996) noted in his commentary on "The Three Assassins of Excellence,"

> [G]iven the economic uncertainty of a world informed by unprecedented change, it is no longer possible for schools to graduate students with sufficient knowledge to respond to the multiple career changes which the student can logically anticipate. (p. 35)

It is also true that the unskilled jobs that provided the backbone of the Industrial Age economy are rapidly disappearing. The fastest-growing sector of the job market involves skilled and technical work that requires the ability to make decisions, work with others, and keep up with rapidly developing technology.

Working in today's economy requires myriad abilities that move beyond, but still include, reading and writing. This is borne out in the SCANS (Secretary's Commission on Achieving Necessary Skills) report, published in 1991 (see fig. I.1 in the Introduction). The report's list of competencies and skills necessary for preparation of the future work force includes—in addition to reading, writing, performing mathematical operations, listening, speaking, and thinking—interpersonal skills, information management, an understanding of systems, and technological literacy.

A Paideia school is designed to engage all students in the development of these competencies and skills. Vocational education is *not* a part of the Paideia curriculum, in the sense that the curriculum does not narrowly train students for specific jobs. This type of vocational education only limits the future of students who take part in it.

The second calling identified by the Paideia Group is to be a good citizen of the nation and the world. A successful democracy requires an informed citizenry of people who share some common fundamental understanding and means through which to communicate. All citizens must have the fundamental skills and disposition required for participation in a democratic nation, including the ability to take responsibility for their own actions, to analyze ideas and act on them, and to communicate effectively with others.

Toward this end, the core curriculum of a Paideia school involves students in constant interaction with the world of ideas. This involvement occurs through their active participation in developing meaningful coached projects and discussing books (not textbooks) and other rich and provocative texts. This type of education provides the foundation for participation in American democracy and acknowledges the special place of the United States in the history of nations.

The United States is a nation chiefly founded upon and bound together by ideas and values, not common ethnicities, languages, or physical borders. Americans are a people of many colors, religions, races, and backgrounds; a nation founded, and primarily populated, by people who left their home nations to seek freedom and a new beginning. Furthermore, the United States is a nation whose major internal difficulties, including one civil war, have resulted from the unequal application of ideas—including democracy, freedom, liberty, and equality. This is certainly true today, when despite a strong economy the United States finds itself with a growing economic disparity between the richest and the poorest of its society, a rapidly increasing prison population, and heightened tensions and conflict among various ethnic groups.

One excellent way to bridge these differences is a rigorous, core curriculum that provides the same quality of education and a common foundation for interaction and communication for all children. Without *the ability to engage in a continuous dialogue regarding the ideas and values of the nation*, the United States will always be at risk of civil disintegration.

To make a good life for one's self is the last of the callings for which school should prepare students, according to the Paideia Group. This goal relates to the aspect of adult life that is personal growth—mental, moral, and spiritual (Adler, 1982, p. 16). To promote lifelong growth, schools should prepare students to recognize and take advantage of opportunities for personal development. The Paideia curriculum helps by creating a system that gives students increasing responsibility and *choice* in developing the means by which they engage in and demonstrate learning.

Answering the Critics

The opportunity for choice is significant because some people use lack of student choice as an argument against a single-track system; however, in a Paideia school students make choices within the curriculum, not regarding design of the curriculum structure itself. As students progress through the grades, the integrated core curriculum gives them an increasing number of choices regarding how to develop, apply, and demonstrate various subject matter.

An example can be seen in Tim Arnold and Damien Bawn's Integrated Humanities (language arts/social studies) course at Federal Hocking High School in Stewart, Ohio. In this class, all students learn how to develop the skills of expository and persuasive writing, historical research, and problem solving while creating real-world coached products. All students in the class are subject to the same standards of quality through the use of a well-developed rubric that incorporates the assessment of both skills developed and knowledge gained. Although the standards are always the same, students and teachers may work out unique ways (for example, different materials, different projects) to achieve the high standard. Through coached projects the students engage in the Paideia curriculum in *meaningful* ways, developing the skills and dispositions of activist learners.

Critics of a core curriculum also cite the difficulty of finding time to fit in electives along with the core courses, a criticism primarily relevant to secondary schools. Two remedies apply. The first is simply to reduce the number of electives offered. The Paideia school is not preparing students for specific tasks; it is preparing them to make decisions over the course of a lifetime. As Adler (1982) notes, "Elective choices are entirely proper at the level of advanced schooling—in our colleges, universities, and technical schools. They are wholly inappropriate at the level of basic schooling" (p. 21). Electives not only result in de facto academic segregation but also will lead some students to voluntarily downgrade their own education (Adler, 1982). The second remedy, simply to let the curriculum determine the schedule, is dealt with in detail in Chapter 6.

Critics have also faulted the core curriculum for promoting monoculturalism. This criticism fails on two counts: by not acknowledging the worth of a shared foundation for understanding and by not distinguishing between transcultural and multicultural subjects. The core curriculum of the Paideia school is intended to enable each student to participate as an active citizen in American society, a society that is the most multicultural democracy in the world. As members of a multicultural society Americans must share a common cultural grounding, one that includes works of excellence from several cultural backgrounds. As E. D. Hirsch (1987) points out in his proposal for cultural literacy, "Literate culture is the most democratic in our land" (p. 21). That is to say, a shared cultural common ground need not be everyone's first culture, but it should be everyone's second and the basis for democratic behavior. An American's first culture is culture of the home and may be predominantly Vietnamese, Greek, Native American, or Appalachian; however, once outside the home, Americans must have a means for all members of the society to live and grow together.

In Atheneum Middle School in Anchorage, Alaska, *all* students have opportunities to build their capacity to wrestle with the most profound works of human thought through participation in Socratic seminars. They read and discuss the ideas of Pascal, William James, Lao Tzu, Einstein, and many others in the context of a very sophisticated culture. These texts are a vital part of the curriculum, not just as a means to develop a shared cultural grounding, but because they further the students' understanding and proficiencies in the core subjects. For example, when students study the circulatory system, they not only conduct experiments and study photos, but they analyze, question, and discuss William Harvey's *On the Motion of the Heart and Blood*. As a result, the students better understand the working of the circulatory system, and they become familiar with the ideas of the person credited with establishing the principles of this understanding. This experience makes the well from which the students formulate and test their own ideas much deeper and richer.

Developing a shared cultural literacy of history, ideas, and language provides a foundation for future living and learning. It is democratic because it enables people to communicate.

The second weakness in the argument that criticizes a core curriculum for promoting monoculturalism is its failure to distinguish between the nature of different disciplines. Religion, social studies, language arts, and fine arts are by nature multicultural, whereas math and science are *transcultural*. That is, the math and science used in Bangladesh are the same as the math and science used in Great Britain; however, the literature and religion of those countries are not. In a recent essay on multiculturalism, Mortimer Adler makes the point that we have no trouble making these distinctions outside of schools—for example, "Chicago is multicultural in its restaurants but not in its hardware stores" (Adler, 1996, p. 9). A literate Chicagoan should understand the history and government of Chicago, which includes some knowledge of the cultures of the various groups that define its population. By extension, a literate American should know more about the history and government of the United States than the history and government of China (though a student should have a basic understanding of China).

One way this distinction is reflected in the curriculum of a Paideia school is through interaction with rich primary sources in Socratic seminars. For example, in history, while the students should read and discuss the "Gettysburg Address," the "Declaration of Independence," and "Letter From Birmingham Jail," they should also read and discuss China's *Book of Odes*. The criteria for text selection are that they be classic, primary, and rich. In the Paideia curriculum, *classic* means transcultural and timeless and refers to works that allow students to participate in what Robert Hutchins (1952) termed "The Great Conversation."

Paideia educators believe classics should inform the education of all students because such works are by definition the repository of any culture's best thought and most profound feeling about the human condition. The core curriculum of the Paideia school is very close to what Hutchins terms a "liberal education," an education steeped in the great works of a culture. He says clearly that "the aim of liberal education is human excellence, both private and public" (p. 3). He goes on to write that

> the liberally educated man is at home in the world of ideas and in the world of practical affairs, too, because he understands the relation of the two. . . . He may even derive from his liberal education some conception of the difference between a bad world and a good one and some notion of the ways in which one might be turned into the other. (p. 4)

In sum, Paideia education is the marriage of two seemingly contradictory ideas—intellectual rigor and equal access to a quality education—and will allow us to heed the wisdom of Thomas Jefferson when he said, "If a nation expects to be ignorant and free, in a state of civilization, it expects what never was and never will be." The core curriculum of a rigorous liberal education empowers the students, faculty, and staff of a school to accomplish the ultimate goals of schooling: virtue, generosity, and right action, not just employability or high test scores.

FLEXIBLE SCHEDULING

Lois Johnson

The Paideia school allows curriculum needs to shape scheduling, and scheduling flexibility is the rule rather than the exception.

In its 1994 report entitled *Prisoners of Time*, the National Education Commission on Time and Learning argued that "the fixed clock and calendar is a fundamental design flaw that must be changed," and that "academic time has been stolen to make room for a host of nonacademic activities" (p. 13). This important study highlights a primary reason why reforming teaching practice in many American schools has proven so difficult. Simply put, different and more powerful teaching strategies require different— sometimes radically different—and more flexible scheduling.

One of the most powerful shifts precipitated by Mortimer Adler's original work involves reimagining students so that they are seen not solely in terms of attending "classes" but rather in terms of their participating in various seminar groups, working on coached project teams, and attending high-quality lectures. Another way of thinking about this is to redefine each and every "class" meeting as one of these three types of learning experience so that teacher and student alike understand clearly what their roles are and can prepare accordingly.

Because didactic lessons place students in a passive position, they should last no longer than 20 to 30 minutes. Effective middle school and high school seminars require up to 90 minutes, and some sophisticated coached projects can benefit from even longer blocks of uninterrupted time. The key to empowering teachers to use these more effective strategies is not just redesigning the weekly schedule to meet instructional needs; it also involves building enough flexibility into new schedules to meet the needs of teachers and students planning and implementing individual units of study.

In addition, providing a rigorous classical education for all students may require extending and redesigning the school year as well as the school day to provide ample opportunity both for a rich core curriculum and for keeping all students on track as they progress through that curriculum. Rethinking the use of time in any school environment involves not just carving up the traditional school day, week, or year into different segments but also expanding and reinventing the traditional units themselves. For that reason, schools like the Cason Lane Academy in Murfreesboro, Tennessee, represent not just the future of classical education but the future of American public education in general. Cason has extended the school day, staggered arrival times for teachers, and added optional enrichment programs.

Elementary School Scheduling

Self-contained elementary classrooms offer significant flexibility on a daily basis because the teacher can control the instructional time. Difficulties sometimes arise, however, because of resource classes and special pull-out programs. In some schools teachers circumvent these problems by establishing a core instructional block that is held inviolate; for example, nothing is permitted to intrude from 8:00 a.m. to 11:30 a.m. Teachers and students then have the freedom to use that block of time every day for the most appropriate learning experiences.

At Cason Lane Academy the morning core instructional time is uninterrupted, and resource teachers do not even arrive until 11:00 a.m. Within the core block of time, Cason Lane teachers can schedule short didactic lessons and longer, more involved coached projects that integrate the subject areas.

To staff both the core curriculum block and a highly successful school enrichment program that runs until 6:00 p.m., Cason Lane employees work a variety of flexible schedules. Through judicious use of part-time aides, Cason Lane even has flexible schedules for academic teachers, permitting them to leave at 11:30 a.m. for nine weeks, so they can return those hours to the school by teaching in the enrichment program during another nine-week period. In 1996–97 more than 600 of Cason Lane's approximately 900 students were enrolled in this optional academic enrichment program, working in classes before and after the core instructional block.

Another innovative use of time was designed at Brentmoor Elementary School in Mentor, Ohio, where Principal George Jaroscak and his faculty created the Fine Arts Impact Team (art, music, and physical education resource teachers). These teachers plan with each grade level, basing their combined work with students on the grade-level curriculum and interacting with each grade level for up to two and a half hours one day a week. The result is a comprehensive fine arts project at each grade level that closely supports academic instruction in the "regular" classroom.

Middle School Scheduling

The middle school concept is ideally suited to flexible scheduling: the team of four core curriculum teachers typically has a block of time that can be adjusted almost weekly to incorporate the various tasks each has to accomplish. Through daily joint planning, interdisciplinary lessons, and cooperative effort, teachers can manipulate their own time and that of students to everyone's best advantage. Interdisciplinary lessons have the added benefit of helping students see the relationships among all the academic subjects as well as permitting focused attention on coached projects that can be worked on during a common block of time. A single project can be assessed in each classroom without the student having to prepare something different for each teacher. The student spends time on a high-quality effort rather than on four different assignments that have no continuity or balance. Working in this way, the student begins to experience the satisfaction of producing something of great inherent value, of working at a level of deep understanding rather than "covering" and memorizing material that may be forgotten soon after the test is taken.

Paideia teachers at Githens Middle School in Durham, North Carolina, for example, developed fully integrated units on *justice* as a core theme, asking students to contribute to a number of coached projects as well as participate in a series of seminars on classical texts ranging from the Ten Commandments to speeches by Martin Luther King. Eventually these units were coordinated into a schoolwide thematic focus. Sixth graders explored the question, "What Is Justice?"; 7th graders considered, "How Has Justice Evolved?"; and 8th graders questioned "Whether Perfect Justice Is Possible in Human Society." Flexible scheduling by teams of teachers and students at all three grade levels made this type of integrated study possible.

High School Scheduling

Most traditional high schools have divided the school day into six, seven, or eight 40- to 60-minute periods. This schedule was clearly designed for administrative ease in planning, not for providing ample time for a variety of powerful teaching techniques. During the past 20 years, however, educators have created a variety of options for secondary schools that are much more sensitive to instructional needs. Among these are modular and block scheduling.

Modular Scheduling

A typical modular schedule allows for 18 modules, 20 minutes in length, each day. These can then be distributed according to the needs of a particular subject or instructional strategy (see fig. 6.1).

For example, physical education might be held only on Monday, Wednesday, and Friday, with each class taking four to six modules. This reduces substantially the amount of time lost in "dressing in and out." A similar schedule for vocational education minimizes time lost traveling to and from a job site, setting up equipment, and cleaning up, while allowing the maximum amount of time for actual work on "live" projects. A science teacher might opt for three modules per class on Monday and Tuesday, providing ample time for a short didactic introduction followed by the organization of research teams for a coached project; one module on Thursday for lab preparation; and four modules on Friday for laboratory experiments. The language arts teacher might request two modules on

FIGURE 6.1
A Typical Modular Schedule

	Monday	Tuesday	Wednesday	Thursday	Friday
1	Science *Didactic Project Planning*	Science *Coached Projects*	Language Arts *Coached Projects*	Science *Lab Prep.*	Foreign Language *Seminar*
2					
3					
4	Foreign Language *Didactic*		Math Lab *Coached Projects and/or Seminar*	Physical Education *Didactic and Coached Projects*	Math *Didactic Project Planning*
5					
6	Language Arts *Didactic*	Physical Education *Didactic and Coached Projects*			
7					
8	Math Lab *Coached Projects*			Social Studies *Didactic*	Lunch
9			Foreign Language *Coached Projects*		
10				Foreign Language *Coached Projects*	Language Arts *Seminar and/or Coached Projects*
11					
12		Lunch	Lunch		
13	Lunch			Lunch	
14		Social Studies *Coached Projects*	Social Studies *Coached Projects*		
15				Language Arts *Didactic and Coached Projects*	Science *Coached Laboratory Experiments or Seminar*
16	Social Studies *Seminar*				
17					
18		Foreign Language *Didactic*	U.T.*		

*Unstructured Time (U.T.) is used for help sessions with subject area teachers or independent study in the media center.

Monday and Wednesday—for short didactic presentations and small-group activity planning—four modules on Thursday for seminar, and three on Friday for coached project work planned earlier in the week. The social studies teacher might choose a four-module framework on Mondays for research and coached project work, two modules on Tuesday and Wednesday for didactic lessons and project planning, and five on Thursday for coached project work or seminars. The foreign language teacher might request two modules per day on Monday and Tuesday, with three on Thursday and Friday for seminars and coached projects.

The flexibility of this schedule not only allows but also encourages the integration of the various "disciplines" that make up the core classical curriculum. High school teachers move naturally from planning together to teaching together in thematic units that emphasize the conceptual relationships between the subject areas.

Students often adapt to the flexible schedule more easily than teachers who have a long history of daily 50-minute periods. Typically, the flexible schedule remains the same each week; some schools rearrange the modules weekly, giving students a new schedule each Monday morning. In either case, the goal is to schedule according to the chronological needs of each teaching and learning "event," not the dictates of the traditional model.

Block Scheduling

An increasing number of high schools are choosing to follow a schedule made up of longer blocks of instructional time. Under block scheduling the student typically has four classes, each approximately 90 minutes long. In the two most popular forms of block scheduling, students take either four classes each day for a semester, or eight classes—four each on alternating days—for a year (see fig. 6.2).

The semester block schedule allows students to complete a course in a semester for one credit. The advantage is that the students have to deal with only four classes each semester as opposed to six or seven classes in the traditional schedule. An added advantage is that at any one time the teacher has only 75 to 100 students in classes of 25 each, allowing for much more personal attention. Traditional scheduling generally requires that teachers cope with 120 to 175 students each day. Administratively, the block schedule results in financial savings because over the year, the teacher can work with up to 200 students. The primary concern with this form of block scheduling is that students complete a class three or four months before standardized testing usually takes place. This is a particular concern for Advanced Placement students, but AP testing may soon be offered twice a year to accommodate students completing coursework at midyear.

FIGURE 6.2
A Typical Block Schedule

	Period	Monday	Tuesday	Wednesday	Thursday	Friday
		Alternate Day or 1st Semester Block				
All Periods 90 Minutes	1	Language Arts				→
	2	Social Studies				→
	3	Physical Education				→
	4	Fine Arts				→

	Period	Monday	Tuesday	Wednesday	Thursday	Friday
		Alternate Day or 2nd Semester Block				
All Periods 90 Minutes	1	Math				→
	2	Elective or Internship				→
	3	Science				→
	4	Foreign Language				→

After initiating this form of block scheduling, Andrew Jackson High School in Jacksonville, Florida, has experienced a number of positive changes. Grades are improving and the number of behavior referrals is dropping, probably because students make fewer class changes and because the longer class periods permit more student-involved coached projects and seminars.

With alternate-day block scheduling, a student has different classes on alternate days and is enrolled in all classes for the full year. This plan retains all the advantages of longer instructional blocks and allows students to take classes through the spring testing period.

Under either plan, teachers have discovered that they must alter delivery of instruction because neither they nor the students can bear 90-minute lectures. The longer period not only provides time for coached projects and evocative seminars, it is actually untenable without more student-centered teaching. Students must play an active role.

Changes in the Calendar

Systemic Paideia reform often involves reforming the calendar as well as the daily schedule. Year-round schooling is a major change being tried around the United States. Although the impetus for a year-round schedule has been primarily to increase the number of students that a school can contain, many schools have adopted a year-round schedule because they believe it provides a number of benefits to students.

In a single-track, year-round program students attend school for 12 weeks and are off for 3, with all students having at least 3 weeks off in July. Many teachers working on a traditional calendar report that they have to spend at least 6 weeks on review work after a long summer break. Teachers on the year-round single track indicate that they need only a day or two for review after each 3-week break before beginning new material. In addition, the year-round, single-track school usually provides a week or more of accelerated instruction during the 3-week intercession for students who are lagging behind. This means that slower students do not wait until they have concluded a year's work before receiving the tutoring they need to thrive in a rigorous academic program.

Creating a classical school that will adequately prepare students for life in the 21st century requires that we revise our traditional ideas about the school day, week, and year for at least three reasons. First, to teach a strong, comprehensive curriculum to all students requires a core block of instructional time. Second, to help all students reach rigorous annual benchmarks in a demanding core curriculum, we need the calendar flexibility to teach some students up to 210 days per year. Finally, to create true lifelong learners, we have to erase the old notion that learning is limited to a 6-hour day, a 5-day week, or a 180-day agrarian year. Children should grow into adulthood with the habit of mind that learning is a continuous, unbroken path that extends through life.

INTEGRATING THE ARTS
Gail Gellatly

A Paideia school should educate students across a wide range of intelligences. All students should be nurtured in fine arts, movement, music, and the manual arts and given the opportunity to explore these areas as they relate to core academic subjects.

A well-rounded liberal arts education is the goal of the Paideia school. Appreciation for and participation in the fine and manual arts are an integral part of building the foundation for a lifetime of learning and cultural enrichment. When we use the phrase "educating students across a wide range of intelligences," we refer to the categorization of learning modes such as Howard Gardner's (1983) groupings of musical, spatial, bodily-kinesthetic, personal, logical-mathematical, and linguistic intelligences. Gardner himself says that "there can never be a single irrefutable and universally accepted list of human intelligences" (p. 60), but Paideia educators maintain that awareness of the different ways in which people learn and especially the ways in which they excel is essential to powerful teaching.

Gardner theorizes that

> individuals are not all alike in their cognitive potentials and their intellectual styles and that education can be more properly carried out if it is tailored to the abilities and the needs of the particular individuals involved. Indeed, the cost of attempting to treat all individuals the same, or of trying to convey knowledge to individuals in ways uncongenial to their preferred modes of learning, may be great. (p. 60)

Because students vary in potential and learning styles, exposing them to a variety of experiences that call upon the use of different intelligences provides more equitable access to learning. Although teachers often balk at the suggestion that students' needs must be addressed individually, exposing them to many different forms of learning experiences not only broadens the potential for receptivity but also allows for blending of intelligences. For example, the revolutionary educator Maria Montessori championed the idea of learning through the senses and devoted herself to the development of educational materials that would seize upon the child's innate kinesthetic and spatial intelligence.

The Essential Element for the arts relates to one of the Paideia Group's original principles: "Schooling at its best is preparation for becoming generally educated in the course of a whole lifetime, and schools should be judged on how well they provide such preparation." In the "Fine Arts" chapter of *The Paideia Program*, John Van Doren (1984) writes that the most important of the three lifetime objectives of Paideia is "the making of a good human life for oneself. . . . [This] cannot be achieved unless the fine arts play a part in it" (p. 151).

As Van Doren recommends, "The fine arts program, which has a tendency to become specialized, should be as fully integrated as possible" with the work in the liberal and manual arts (p. 148). A classical education is founded on the notion that by attaining a certain degree of mastery in all subjects, continuing one's learning becomes a natural part of living one's life after formal schooling ends. Basic music theory, general theories of design and color, an appreciation for the great masters of painting as well as for ballet, all serve as cultural foundations for integrating the arts into a framework of cultural literacy.

Unfortunately, many schools in the United States today do not view the arts as a necessary part of the curriculum. According to Edward Miller (1994),

> in spite of the fact that scholars and educators from Jerome Bruner and Elliott Eisner to Maxine Greene and Howard Gardner have argued for years that the arts are essential to children's development and should be valued equally with core subjects . . . arts education remains near the bottom of the list of curricular priorities in most school districts. It is seen

as a frill, or as "enrichment" for the talented few. . . . Underlying the struggle to promote arts education in U.S. public schools is widespread doubt about how many kids really benefit from such classes. Few educators take the position that the slogan "all children can learn" applies to drawing, singing, writing plays, and playing the violin. Yet the experience of individual teachers offers persuasive evidence that we may be vastly underestimating the potential of many children. (p. 7)

Most schools will continue to teach the arts as separate subjects, allowing students with interest or talent in the arts to develop their skills. However, schools are encouraged to form art teams or interdisciplinary teams that allow teachers of the arts to coordinate with other subject-area teachers on projects. Teachers need to plan together to integrate the arts into units on mathematics, history, and other subjects.

Three-Column Teaching and the Arts

The Paideia program's three-column approach is well suited to an integrated study of the arts. For example, music teachers may present ideas in the didactic mode to address such areas as music theory, historical background of composers and musical forms, instruction on active listening, the basics of composition, and the use of an instrument (including the voice). The coaching of individual musical skills, as well as group efforts (such as chorus or orchestra), builds on the foundation laid in the didactic phase. Teachers coach students who are conducting research on a composer as well as those who are developing a composition or analyzing an existing piece. Students can then participate in a music seminar as a culminating activity following the study of a particular piece of music, a composer, or a lesson in composition. A seminar by members of the chorus after a performance can serve as both a self-critique and an exploration of the music itself and how the students responded to performing it. Music seminars can also be valuable as an introduction to a unit of study, a way of generating student interest in further investigation.

As with music, teachers can introduce the fine arts didactically and then coach student understanding and skill in product-oriented projects. A brief lecture on the qualities of color, light, and design serves as a springboard for individual artistic expression. The art instructor may coach a student in the use of certain materials or in implementing a particular design or craft. The enrichment that seminars bring to the study of art cannot be overstated. Students can discuss their own paintings, drawings, or sculptures, or the seminar can be based on a recognized classical work. A teacher may chose to illuminate a particular aspect of art, for example color, by scheduling a seminar on Mondrian, either at the beginning of the unit, after the initial didactic lesson, or as a culminating activity at the end. A seminar upon completion of a class mural project can bring many aspects of the process into play: students can consider how they represented ideas through the various techniques in which they had been coached, and they can reflect on not only what they learned but also the learning process itself.

The seminar is a powerful tool for investigating any classical work of art. It not only creates a natural spawning ground for the exchange of great ideas (the backbone of any seminar discussion), but provides the chance for an infusion of individual experience, adding personal meaning to a classical work that has engaged humanity through the ages. Students who view a slide of Richard Westall's painting *The Sword of Damocles* (1812) may discuss any of the following themes: power, responsibility, monarchy, wisdom, government, and judgment (see fig. 7.1).

At first glance, it may seem that the manual arts—carpentry, masonry, mechanics, drafting, and design, for example—are neither an integral part of a classical curriculum nor amenable to three-column teaching. However, upon closer scrutiny, it becomes clear that they should be a natural, integrated part of every child's learning because they instruct and enhance visual, spatial, and kinesthetic intelligence. Further, the manual arts teach motor skills in the context of applied concepts, allowing students to build on their own ideas—specifically those that flow of out of their study of the core curriculum. For example, students at a rural high school might get involved in the movement to save and restore a 200-year-old log cabin as part of their survey of local historical structures. Discovering that the cabin must be moved to be saved, they receive permission to restore it on school property. At this point, their study of history, carpentry, drafting, and

FIGURE 7.1
The Seminar Is a Powerful Tool
for Studying Classical Works of Art

Richard Westall, British, 1765–1836, "The Sword of Damocles," oil on canvas, 1812. Reproduced with permission from Ackland Art Museum, The University of North Carolina at Chapel Hill, Ackland Fund.

architecture merge as they work with an expert in historical renovation to dismantle, move, and reconstruct the cabin. To complete this project, they will need expert didactic instruction and coaching from several sources, including teachers. Ultimately, their completed structure should precipitate a seminar that might focus on the primary concepts surrounding human shelter and how it reflects or nurtures family and community. The point here is that manual skills are a vital part of any truly empowering education, and, for some students, they represent the best entrée to the study of more "academic" subjects.

In physical education, teachers introduce the basic skills and rules of a game or dance pattern, and students then practice what they have been taught under the guidance of the coach/teacher. Seminars can follow a game or a dance performance or the viewing of a video of a game, classic ballet, or folk dance. Learning about how the human body functions can deepen students' awareness of what they are learning and lead to a more holistic grasp of physical movement. A didactic lesson on the structure of the human body can lead to a seminar on human anatomy. A seminar on the skeleton, for example, can serve as the culmination of many different kinds of lessons, particularly when one considers that the concepts of structure, flexibility, and range of motion are all fundamental ideas.

Links with Other Subjects

Although the arts disciplines can fall neatly into self-contained units of study, integrating them into the core subjects is an important albeit challenging goal, given the reality of schedules and course requirements. Integrating the arts into the core curriculum adds interest and relevance to the study of any culture and brings learning to life in a way that broadens the depth of meaning. Consider the degree to which studying the European Renaissance is enriched by including the literature, music, art, and dance of the time. Studying ancient Greece might include the building of a middle-class Athenian home, an Olympics unit in P.E., or the production of a Greek play. In *The Paideia Program* Van Doren (1984) writes:

Should anybody wonder what a class in mathematics can have to do with painting, let Cézanne's remark be recalled when he said that the painter sees all objects in terms of their geometry. In music, anyone can hear the intervals and learn from the physics of sound how deviations from strict ratios have permitted what we call harmony. So with other subjects such as history and language. Students who are reading *Hamlet* should take it for granted that their schooling will extend from reading the play to speaking it aloud, seeing it performed, acting in it, and possibly giving time to making scenery for its production. (p. 148)

If we were to walk into a Paideia school and look for indicators that the "arts elements" were in place, we would look for involvement of all children in regular music, dance or athletics, manual arts and visual arts, as well as the integration of these disciplines into the core subjects. At Brentmoor Elementary in Mentor, Ohio, students don't go to separate art, music, and physical education classes (often referred to as "specials"), but rather to "Fine Arts" once a week for two hours. The Fine Arts Impact Team consists of teachers in vocal and instrumental music, movement (P.E.), and the visual arts. The two-hour block allows for greater flexibility in team teaching and more opportunity for interdisciplinary learning, as well as joint projects.

Cindy Sawchick, art teacher at Brentmoor, describes how the team uses an interdisciplinary approach not only to weave the arts (including movement) together, but also to integrate them into the core subjects. She cites the example of a program the children produced culminating their studies in science and art that conveyed the idea of cycles (night and day, darkness and light):

The exhibition "TIME" involved all students in grades 2–6 and revealed the interconnectedness between core subjects and the fine arts. TIME was represented by two formal art elements, circle and line. The 4th grade class assembled on stage in the darkness to "The Music of the Night" and opened the audience's eyes to white light and its prismatic refraction through circular and linear formations and movements. Art, movement, and music conveyed the magic of rainbows. Students, dressed in white, moved from a linear band of white light into a prism formation. Others dressed in various colors traveled through the prism and dispersed into linear bands of color, forming a rainbow. All the students then filed into a circular formation to the music "Somewhere Over the Rainbow," assembling themselves in the order of the color wheel. Next, they paired up with their complementary-color partner to show color relationships. The effect was enhanced by a round dance during which each student's art work was projected on stage and intertwined with a color skit illustrating the lyrics to the song. (1995, p. 4)

These students gained an understanding of the scientific concepts of color, light, and time in a way that was experientially rich, especially when compared with learning it from a textbook or from a teacher's lecture. When students use the arts as a vehicle to present what they have learned, not only do they integrate the disciplines, but they also enhance their ownership of learning by incorporating it into highly personal, creative expression.

Schools can benefit from the participation of local artists, becoming "a place of interest to people of talent in the community, people whose encouragement and support will make not only its fine arts program but the whole Paideia undertaking easier than it would otherwise be" (Van Doren, 1984, p. 152). Community involvement is an integral part of the success of a Paideia school, and the synergy created by networking a diverse group of talented individuals can nourish the school's arts program in mutually beneficial ways for all involved. Thus, appreciation of and participation in the arts foster a sense of community, as well as a grasp of past civilizations and the multiple cultures of today's world. "The arts are what give perspective to an understanding of history and literature and, indeed, culture generally. Without the arts no study of any culture is complete," argues A. Graham Down, President Emeritus of the Council for Basic Education (n.d.).

Artistic works must be thought of as cultural statements. Creative expression is a vital part of "The Great Conversation" championed by Robert Hutchins (1952):

The kind of things that are most intelligible and most revealing are ideas and artistic objects. They are most readily understood; they are most characteristic of the peoples who have produced or stated them. We can learn more about another people from their artistic and intellectual productions than we can from all the statistics and data that can ever be collected. (pp. 63–64)

The classical ideal is that of a strong mind complemented by a strong body. The notion of multiple intelligences enhances this ancient idea by adding to the sum a strong social intelligence—in other words, a strong heart. To achieve this ideal, however, we must educate the entire child by allowing students to exercise their full range of abilities and so to realize the richness of all their inherited potential.

ASSESSMENT

Laura Billings and Terry Roberts

In a Paideia school, assessment of students and teachers is individualized rather than standardized—emphasizing portfolio and narrative assessments rather than traditional grading and appraisal. Individual growth is always stressed.

In a Paideia classroom, the defining characteristics of assessment are evident both in the rationale behind testing and the variety of grading methods used. Homework, class work, and quizzes are still translated into letter grades and report cards, but the reason teachers use these traditional tools is to communicate students' progress. Paideia teachers typically go further to help parents and students by providing "report cards [that] are . . . [designed] to keep the focus on students' individual achievement and effort by including personalized teacher narratives and reports on cumulative student progress that do not compare students or assign ranking orders within classes" (Wheelock, 1994, p. 89). Traditional methods are used in the Paideia classroom to facilitate teaching and learning, not to control student behavior or emphasize teacher power. In addition, Paideia teachers often use checklists, rubrics, portfolios, and narrative assessments to provide more extensive, individualized feedback and involve students in the assessment effort.

In a Paideia classroom the three columns of instruction—didactic, coaching, and seminar—and the results thereof—knowledge, skill, and understanding—guide the teaching and learning process. Because different types of instruction facilitate different modes of learning, so do different forms of assessment illuminate different forms of progress and performance.

Assessment in the Paideia classroom is an integral part of the teaching process—an ongoing, cyclical process.

Teaching-Assessment Cycle

The teaching-assessment cycle includes the following steps: (1) determine the goal and objectives, (2) identify students' status in relation to the goal and objectives, (3) progress toward the goal, (4) measure the progress. Teacher and students then begin the cycle over again by determining the new goal and objectives (see fig. 8.1).

FIGURE 8.1
The Cycle of Assessment

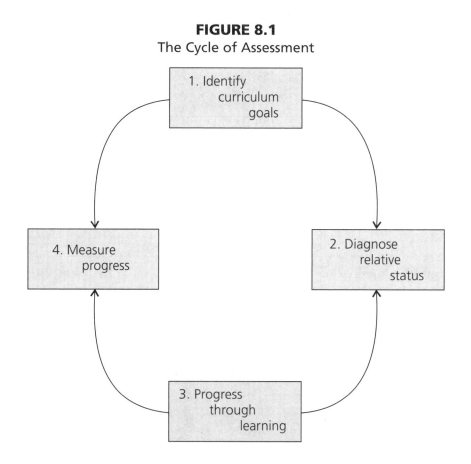

Step 1. Determining the goal. To model democratic education, a Paideia teacher begins by discussing the course goals and objectives with students. These course objectives—say, in a 7th grade language arts class—are often set forth by state or local curriculums, but they should not be confused with standardized tests, nor should they be derived from the table of contents of an adopted textbook. The 7th grade language arts teacher can facilitate a useful discussion with students by categorizing these objectives into general groups (e.g. reading, writing, listening, speaking). Taking time with students to discuss the goals of the course allows time for clarification of purpose and relevancy. This discussion helps students see usefulness in the endeavor and, likewise, challenges teachers to a relevance check on what they intend for students to do. Finally, the teacher should facilitate some semblance of consensus and put discussed goal and objectives into a detailed syllabus or action plan.

This discussion with students is the foundational work for the school year, the semester, or the unit. In addition to the goal and objectives, teacher and students should discuss a fair, effective process for achieving these. As the goals and objectives are put into an action plan, consensus about the process should be formulated into class rules or individual contracts if need be. Throughout the unit, semester, or school year, teacher and students revisit what they agreed upon during the original goal-setting conversation. This process creates an optimal blending of curriculum and instruction, course goals and classroom management, teacher wisdom and student enthusiasm.

Step 2. Identifying students' status in relation to the goal and objectives. This step can be accomplished through a variety of pre-tests or diagnostics. While the method or instrument used is important, the imperative is that teachers take time to figure out where students are before launching into a unit of instruction. Admittedly, this requires a good deal of flexibility on the part of the teacher. However, in a Paideia classroom, student learning is paramount and thus individual status drives the instruction.

Step 3. Progressing toward the goal. Teachers and students engage in processing information, developing skills, and fostering understanding through succinct didactic lessons, ongoing coached work, and thoughtful seminars.

Step 4. Measuring progress and performance. The measurement step illuminates for students (and parents, administrators, etc.) the progress that has been made. Likewise, this information clarifies the progress yet to be made. This final step—often where evaluation takes place—illuminates the teacher-student relationship in a Paideia classroom. Because a Paideia teacher focuses on student knowledge via didactic instruction, collaborative effort in project development, and discussion of ideas during seminar, this final step of measuring progress unfolds in myriad ways with collaboration among various participants.

Assessing Didactic Instruction

Step 1. Discussing goals and objectives in terms of didactic instruction is often based on the coached project. As discussed in Chapter 4, the Paideia teacher discusses with students the factual knowledge necessary for accuracy in products and performances. The goals and objectives of didactic instruction are also discussed and selected in conjunction with seminar texts.

Step 2. Identifying student status in relation to factual knowledge can occur through a brief conversation, a multiple-choice test, or a project design assignment. A Paideia teacher constructs some types of diagnostic activity to derive baseline information for each goal and objective. For example, students may be asked to explain the parts of a paragraph in language arts, identify the segments of the color wheel in art, label the parts of a cell in biology. Baseline assessment for didactic instruction sets the direction for collaborative teaching and learning.

Step 3: Progressing toward the goals and objectives. Didactic instruction means disseminating information through a number of teacher-centered methods previously discussed in Chapter 4.

Step 4: Measuring the results of didactic instruction is what most traditional forms of evaluation are designed to do. Factual information is efficiently displayed through multiple-choice and short-answer tests and fill-in-the-blank quizzes. A grade book is the natural place for such information to be recorded, but it should also be part of the individual student's notebook or portfolio. Collaboration, clarity, and no surprises are key to completion of the cycle and beginning new goals with eagerness, trust, and respect.

Step 1 then happens again. Paideia teachers use the traditional pattern of teaching, testing, and reteaching because this cycle indicates to the teacher what information needs to be reviewed or presented in a different way. Assessment signals the need for more work in a particular area—both on the part of students and teacher. Assessment activities allow all involved to measure progress and to collaboratively determine pace and direction.

Assessing Coached Projects

Step 1: Determining the goals of a coached project. As evident in the description of the project in Chapter 3, the second column of instruction involves extensive teacher and student planning. The project goals and objectives are often documented in checklists and timelines so all involved can easily see the common goal. The numerous intellectual skills involved in a coached project are frequently discussed and displayed on calendars and in rubric form. Often Paideia teachers and students plan backwards from the product or performance to expedite the development of detailed work plans and timelines.

Step 2: Identifying student status in relation to the skills of the coached project. Based on the list of skills needed to carry out the project, teacher and students identify strengths and weaknesses in myriad areas: for example writing, calculating, and building.

Step 3: Progressing toward the goals and objectives of a coached project. In the Paideia classroom, a coached project includes specific content skills, yet naturally integrates many content areas. Progress toward the goals and objectives, therefore, is guided by the project description, but flexible enough to include a variety of ways of succeeding at a subject. The teacher is head coach, yet students consistently coach one another as well. Students are assigned different responsibilities, yet the work is demanding in an effort to achieve the agreed-upon goal, not to meet arbitrary quotas, as Grant Wiggins (1993) advises. Different groups work with specialized checklists on specific group responsibilities. The common factor communicated to all is: effort, follow through, attention to quality, and timeliness.

Step 4: Measuring progress in the coached project. Having taken the time in Step 1 to describe in detail the goals and objectives of the coached project, measuring them is a matter of taking note of where everyone is in relation to the desired end. The checklists and timelines often evolve into narratives and rubrics. Students produce both oral and written reports of their progress. At Madison Elementary, the students' written work is displayed in an information pamphlet placed in the local museum and is, therefore, assessed by a wide audience. Students display their constructions, describe their accomplishments, or perform their skills in front of real audiences, which include their teacher and parents, but also their fellow students, students down the hall, and community members outside the school building. Often, these efforts shape into a portfolio illuminating progress and creativity. All methods of assessing progress in the coached project focus on both individual and group progress.

Student assessment during a coached project is largely ongoing and involves students assessing their own performance as well as that of others. As a model for such collaboration, teachers also help one another assess student progress. Damien Bawn and Tim Arnold of Federal Hocking High School in Stewart, Ohio, consistently model this process. For each coached project in their English and social studies classes, they work with students to create a project evaluation sheet specific to that project. Students score points for each stage of their participation, so that they are witness to and responsible for their progress, and the end result is a "grade" for their participation in the entire project.

In the example in Figure 8.2, students in 11th grade American literature and history classes are creating colonial newspapers as their coached products, drawing on a variety of content material to produce articles, advertisements, even political cartoons. They score points toward their final "grade" individually and as group members. Teachers fill in some of these scores on their own, some in collaboration with students, and have students self-assess in some areas. The focus is on rewarding all parts of student involvement in the project and creating a lot of dialogue about quality. This sort of collaborative assessment honors both the need for process and a "grade" as the product of that process.

Teacher Self-Assessment and the Coached Project

Unlike either a lecture or a seminar, a coached project is a much more complex teaching and learning event that takes a number of class sessions to complete. Learning to lead coached projects often requires teachers to redesign the fundamental organization of their classroom as well as what and how they teach. As a result, teachers in Paideia schools have been most successful in managing this transition when they were able to support one another as colleagues, visiting one another's classrooms as "peer learners," studying the ongoing projects they find there. When one teacher observes another, the observer (or peer learner) should study the work of his or her colleague, gaining insight from the intellectual coaching of students. The "Coached Project Checklist" given in full in Appendix C is designed to structure precisely this sort of collaboration. It is divided into three parts that suggest the visiting teacher interview the teacher/coach, make specific observations about the classroom environment, and interview students at random. Although teachers in Guilford County, North Carolina, and other schools around the country are using this checklist, it should continue to evolve as teachers adapt it to different settings, students, and projects.

FIGURE 8.2
Colonial Paper Project Assessment—The Final Report

Community _____   Colony Represented _____

Student	Community Score	Individual Score	Assignments Missing	Student's Final Score

Overall Comments:
_____
_____

FIGURE 8.2—*(continued)*
Colonial Paper Project Assessment—The Final Report

Community _____   Colony Represented _____

Section/ Assignment		Author Feature	Title	Page #	Comment
Feature News Articles 25 pts each	1 2 3 4 5				
Editorials 15 pts each	1 2				
Letters to the Editor 20 pts each	1 2 3 4 5				
Local News Articles 25 pts each	1 2 3 4 5				
Ads 3 pts each	1 2 3 4 5 6 7 8				
Profile-Leader 15 pts					
Advice Column 8 pts					
Crossword 8 pts					
Comic Strips 5 pts each	1 2				
Editorial Cartoon 5 pts					
Want Ad Section 5 pts					
Special Section 10 pts					
Layout Neatness/ Originality 20 pts					
Penalty for errors					

Seminar Assessment

Step 1: Determining the goals of the seminar, as described in Chapter 2, often occurs as an unfolding process. The Paideia teacher begins setting goals and objectives for the seminars based on students' maturity, previous seminar experience, and knowledge base. As curriculum accumulates and spirals through the years, so do behavioral and cognitive expectations. Interestingly, the seminar is itself a method of assessment for conceptual thinking skills and modes of communication.

The goal of a 1st grade seminar may be to sit still and look at the person speaking. By high school, students will be expected to refer to the text, criticize points thoughtfully, and ask other participants questions. The behaviors identified through a seminar participation rubric should bear a direct relationship to the developmental level of the students (see fig. 8.3).

Step 2: Identifying student status in relation to the goal. In terms of both the discussion process and the basic information required for seminar on a particular text, a Paideia teacher often constructs a type of preseminar activity (e.g., reading a poem and discussing vocabulary and historical context in order to prepare for the actual seminar discussion). In addition, the teacher and students may consider how well students can sit in a circle and talk with one another without raising their hands. Student status in relation to speaking, listening, and thinking should be given serious consideration and extensive practice before expecting civil and thoughtful classroom dialogue. In identifying students' status in relation to seminar goal and objectives, the Paideia teacher usually focuses the students' attention on a few behavioral objectives at a time.

Step 3: Progressing toward the goals of the seminar. Teachers first learning to lead seminars quickly realize that they have to coach seminar behavior in their students. They come to see that they need to describe the seminar process clearly (often with a model video, checklists, and rubrics) and then stress continual growth toward the ideal. Students come to see that individually and as a group they must continually mature their seminar skills. Paideia teachers understand that grading seminar participation as a way to ensure student involvement nullifies the trust and respect desirable in the seminar process. "Grades keep score of the amount of information and

FIGURE 8.3
Paideia Seminar Participation Rubric

CONDUCT	LISTENING
Student sits seminar style.	Student looks at person who is speaking.
Student looks at person talking and listens to learn.	Student asks questions about what has been said.
Student waits for turn to speak.	Student talks about what he or she has heard.
Student is polite.	
1 2 3 4 5	1 2 3 4 5
SPEAKING	**CRITICAL THINKING**
Student speaks clearly with appropriate voice level.	The student's response reflects listening to the text and going beyond the text.
Student expresses complete thoughts.	The student's response reflects listening to others.
Student's comments relate to the text, questions, or previous statements.	Student can explain why he or she disagrees with another student and can support it from the text.
Student's comments show respect for self and others.	Student response reflects comprehension of text; answers are sought out.
Student asks questions.	Student makes statements that indicate application to real world applications.
1 2 3 4 5	1 2 3 4 5

1 = not yet   2 = occasionally   3 = often   4 = frequently   5 = always

knowledge . . . a smaller part measures the degree of skill . . . little or none measures students' understanding" (National Paideia Center, 1988, p. 180). Students usually improve their progress toward model seminars in fits and starts as many variables collide—students' mood and energy, interest in text, time of year, time of day, or teacher facilitation.

Step 4: Measuring the progress of seminars should occur immediately after the seminar in writing and in further discussion. The postseminar activity or debriefing period works well when independent writing, drawing, and thinking occurs first and then, more discussion—first through self-assessment, then from feedback from others. Figure 8.4 provides some seminar reflection questions. As Earl and LeMahieu suggest: "If students are to become critical thinkers and problem solvers who can bring their talents and knowledge to bear on a particular problem, then developing such skills of self-assessment and self-judgment is essential" (1997, p. 154).

In conjunction with assessing the seminar process, students work on assignments that extend the ideas from the seminar text.

Often seminars generate intriguing questions that are not answered, and so research projects naturally emerge and flow into new coached projects. Student checklists and rubrics that reflect student reading level and development are also used in the postseminar stage. For example, see the elementary grades checklist (grades K–1) and seminar assessment questionnaire (grades 4–5) from Oak Ridge Elementary school (Guilford County, North Carolina) contained in Figures 8.5 and 8.6.

On the other hand, the secondary rubric that we have enclosed in Appendix C describes five learning behaviors that relate to the student's depth of engagement with the text: critical reading, listening, reasoning, speaking, and writing. This particular rubric is instructive because it was developed by teachers and students working together at the Chattanooga School of Arts and Sciences. Not only is it valuable as a teaching tool when coaching seminar participation, but it also helps teachers and students define quality seminar discussion for the entire school community. In other words, it fosters the process of individual and group improvement in this vital learning event.

FIGURE 8.4
Seminar Reflection Questions

- The goal is to assess the seminar in terms of both process and content—individually and collectively.
- Individual, private, *written* assessment is coupled with collective, public, *oral* assessment.

Preseminar:
1. What did you do to prepare for this seminar?
2. Did you have previous knowledge about this text?
3. What did you expect from this seminar?

Seminar:
1. How did your participation affect the seminar ... the group process?
2. How did the group handle the task of analyzing and evaluating the text?
3. What ideas became more important to you throughout the seminar?
4. How did the participants treat one another?
5. What influence did the facilitator have?

Postseminar
1. Did anything about the seminar bother you?
2. Was the text appropriate and challenging? Why/why not?
3. What will you remember about the seminar?
4. What suggestions would you make to improve the seminar?
5. What do you/we need to work on next time?

Source: The National Paideia Center

Teacher Self-Assessment in Seminar Facilitation

The Seminar Guide (also in Appendix C) developed by Amy Bender, a former staff member of the National Paideia Center, is valuable in another way. Although it also helps to define a quality seminar, this checklist is more specifically useful for teachers engaged in improving their seminar leadership skills. The Seminar Guide was developed over the course of several months drawing on the expertise of a wide variety of seminar leaders from a number of schools. It is probably the instrument most in use across the country by teachers engaged in self-assessment (via videotape) or peer coaching programs.

FIGURE 8.5

OAK RIDGE ELEMENTARY
SEMINAR CHECKLIST FOR KINDERGARTEN/1ST GRADE

SEMINAR RATING CHART FOR _____

NAME

DATE _____

TOPIC/TEXT _____

POSITIVE BEHAVIORS

_____ I read the text with an adult.
_____ I thought before speaking.
_____ I listened to other people share their ideas.
_____ I felt good about speaking in the seminar.
_____ I waited my turn to speak.

NEGATIVE BEHAVIORS

_____ I acted silly and disrupted the seminar.
_____ I did not look at the person speaking.
_____ I did not speak at all.
_____ I talked too much.

It is important to note here that the Seminar Guide should not be used to appraise teacher performance in order to rank or rate that teacher's skills. Because the items in the checklist are not of equal importance, 32 out of 36 affirmative answers does not necessarily reflect a more powerful seminar than another discussion that scored 28 out of 36. Rather, this instrument should be used only as part of an ongoing effort to improve a teacher's skills, either by studying a videotape of a seminar or by studying the performance of another teacher in order to learn from the experience. As Bender's introductory notes suggest, the Seminar Guide is more than just a checklist; the white space on its pages is intended for extensive notes on a particular seminar. Further, several teachers report keeping these notes as a chronological record of the seminars they have led, creating a seminar leadership portfolio for self-study and improvement.

Continuous Communication, Collaboration, and Growth

The common element in all these efforts is their focus on valid, open communication between and among teachers, students, and parents—always with intellectual growth as the goal. For this reason, Paideia teachers are discovering the need to revise the ways in which they communicate with parents about their children's progress, turning increasingly to narratives and portfolios to enhance or replace traditional report cards. For example, many teachers in Paideia schools are developing seminar portfolios for themselves as well as each student in their classrooms. In addition to texts, questions, notes, checklists, and rubrics, these portfolios often contain a record sheet like the one in Figure 8.7 to represent graphically the growing seminar skills of an individual student. The items recorded here are described more fully in the seminar rubric used by the class, and students often record their own progress, leading them to accept increasing responsibility for their own learning behavior. This method becomes even more powerful when students are asked to interpret their own seminar portfolios for their parents or other classroom visitors, commenting on their strengths, weaknesses, and—most significantly—their progress.

Exhibiting Mastery

In *Graduation by Exhibition: Assessing Genuine Achievement*, a team of authors led by Joseph P. McDonald included a chapter focused on Sullivan High School in Chicago (1993, pp. 32–47). This chapter, entitled "Socratic

FIGURE 8.6

OAK RIDGE ELEMENTARY
SEMINAR CHECKLIST FOR 4TH/5TH GRADE

SEMINAR RATING CHART FOR _____

NAME

DATE _____

TOPIC/TEXT _____

DIRECTIONS: CIRCLE THE MOST ACCURATE RESPONSE
(N)EVER, (S)OMETIMES, OR (A)LWAYS.

POSITIVE BEHAVIORS

N   S   A   I came prepared for the seminar by reading the text a minimum of three times.
N   S   A   I formulated a possible opening, core, and closing question for this text.
N   S   A   I demonstrated courtesy to others by actively listening and waiting my turn to speak.
N   S   A   I listened to the ideas of others and valued them even when these ideas opposed my own.
N   S   A   I acted as a role model for other students.
N   S   A   I built on what was said before giving my opinion.
N   S   A   I cited examples from the text to validate my opinions. (# cited _____)

NEGATIVE BEHAVIORS

N   S   A   I interrupted others.
N   S   A   I acted silly and disturbed others.
N   S   A   I did not make eye contact with the person speaking.
N   S   A   I did not share any opinions or ideas.
N   S   A   I talked about subjects other than the text.
N   S   A   I talked too much and did not allow others equal time.
N   S   A   I was discourteous to others.

My **personal goal** for improving my seminar participation is

_____

_____

Signature

FIGURE 8.7

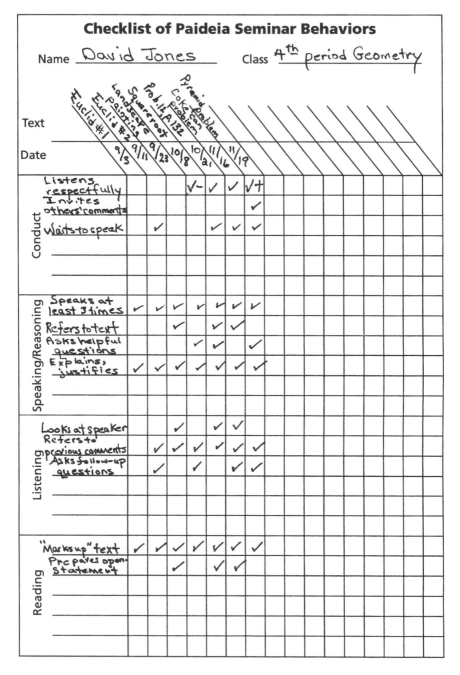

Seminars and Student Essays," describes how beginning in 1989 the faculty at Sullivan, led by then-Principal Robert Brazil, instituted a graduation requirement that they believed appropriate to a Paideia high school: "[B]efore graduating, each . . . [student] would need to demonstrate competence in reading, writing, and thinking by participating in a 90-minute Socratic seminar and by writing an acceptable three- to five-page essay exploring the seminar reading" (pp. 32–33). Two interesting things happened as a result of this decision. First, after what is described as a "volatile debate," the faculty agreed to seminar participation and writing as graduation requirements because they "had invested considerable energy in curriculum reform and wanted evidence of the effectiveness of their efforts" (p. 33). Second,

> As the date of the seminar approached, excitement in the building grew. Seniors, even those most vocally opposed to the exhibition when it was announced, were now heard debating the meaning of Freud's arguments in the hallways. Students who were previously reluctant to take their textbooks to class carried their seminar folders with them everywhere. The manila exhibition folder had become an unspoken symbol of pride among the senior class. (pp. 36–37)

Eventually all but one senior passed the seminar portion of Sullivan's new "exhibition." What is important here is that by changing the way they assessed student ability—even in a "final" exam—the Sullivan High faculty added credibility to the curriculum and teaching reforms they had instituted and altered the climate of the school. The assessment process itself should become a very powerful teaching strategy, whether within a single classroom or an entire school.

Ultimately, traditional forms of evaluation and grading do not suffice because they not only seem like a form of punishment to many students, but they create a schoolwide climate of inequality and finite learning. In other words, traditional grades create a climate fatal to classical education as we define it. In order to prepare students for the 21st century, Paideia schools must stress a rigorous academic education for all students and create in those students the desire and skills for lifelong learning. The rubrics and checklists described here both set a high standard and nurture individual growth toward optimal performance. Furthermore, they stress learning as a continuous process, not a preimposed, standardized curriculum. Assess-ment as we describe it here is an open, dynamic, fluid process that stresses continuous communication, collaboration, and growth—the qualities that define a classically educated *individual* as well as a true learning *community*.

A LIFE DEFINED THROUGH LEARNING

Terry Roberts

Because the goal of schooling is to foster lifelong learning in all those involved, a Paideia school is full of adults and children who view themselves as constantly growing and learning, whose self-assessment is both demanding and fluid.

Educators in the United States have for some time now parroted the phrase "lifelong learning" without providing an operational definition for the term. In fact, the phrase has become so slippery that politicians and policymakers have discovered its usefulness in the public arena; it sounds profound without necessarily meaning anything concrete. Despite the almost trite nature of the phrase, however, arguments abound regarding learning as a lifelong process and schooling as the genesis for that process.

The historical perspective of the 21st century may well view this decade as a fin de siècle period—an age in which we both feared and anticipated the coming century—and an age in which we either succeeded or failed in preparing for that century. Everything we know about the world in which our students will live and work suggests that it will be global in its inclusiveness and volatile in its fluidity; that successive generations of technology will flood even the most private individual's life with information; and that traditional social and civic institutions will come under increasing pressure to evolve. We know, for example, that successful individuals will

• Change careers or paths within careers at a dizzying rate,

- Move freely over the planet (both physically and technologically),
- Form coalitions with a wide variety of people and groups, and
- Aggressively attack problems even as those problems begin to manifest themselves.

They will be, above all else, fluid and dynamic—activist learners.

This profile seems like a new idea, but others have defined a similar individual during equally demanding points in history. As early as 1841, Emerson argued in his essay "Self-Reliance" that

> a sturdy lad from New Hampshire or Vermont, who in turn tries all the professions, who teams it, farms it, peddles, keeps a school, preaches, edits a newspaper, goes to Congress, buys a township, and so forth, in successive years, and always like a cat falls on his feet, is worth a hundred of these city dolls. He walks abreast with his days and feels no shame in not "studying a profession," for he does not postpone his life, but lives already. He has not one chance but a hundred chances. (1979, p. 75)

We might add to our profile of the successful 21st century individual that he or she "always like a cat falls on his [or her] feet."

The fully realized Paideia school is the incubator for this sort of "sturdy" individual, and every learning experience provided in that school contributes to the habits of mind, body, and personality that support this sort of activist life. For this reason, we list the following as characteristic goals under the 14th Essential Element:

- Teacher/parent seminars and symposia,
- Exhibitions and projects created cooperatively by teachers and students,
- Classrooms full of works in progress—those of teachers as well as students, and
- Administrative leaders who are themselves model learners.

We believe that in the 21st century every successful organization will be characterized by learning—both as an organizational value and as a defining characteristic of its members. Thus, the adults in a Paideia school will be potent models for children—enthusiastic and forceful students of the world around them. And as we involve more and more parents and other community members in the activist life of the school, children will grow naturally in a community that values lifelong learning.

Complementary Habits of Lifelong Learning

We may have to replace the common phrase *well-educated* with the less mellifluous but more accurate *well-educating*; to be learned in the 21st century will always involve the present rather than the past tense. The traditional description of the well-rounded individual as a sound mind in a sound body will become rounder still when we consider not only the intellectual and physical attributes that we must learn but also the fact that we must become powerfully self-regulating as well as self-motivating. To prepare children for an adult life defined by continual learning, Paideia schools must teach three sets of complementary habits:

1. *The manipulation and application of information as well as of abstract concepts.* Looking toward the future, it is important to understand that the current debate over teaching information versus skills is based on a dangerously simpleminded and false dichotomy. First, neither can be successfully taught in isolation. Second, in anticipation of the information age, we must teach the coming generations the *skills* needed to select, manipulate, and apply *information*. The 21st century liberal education will produce a student who is technologically and culturally literate; he or she will have carefully read and discussed *King Lear* and will also know how to download selected excerpts from any Shakespeare text from the Internet.

These experiences and skills are not enough, however; that is the point of combining strong didactic and coached instruction with seminar discussion. The classically educated individual must also have wrestled with the ideas and values in Shakespeare's play—pride, prejudice, the evils that corrupt human relations, to name only a few—and so be better able to cope with life on a shrinking planet. If we as the adults in a Paideia school hope to teach the ability to manipulate and apply ideas as well as information, then we must ourselves model and practice what we preach.

2. The habit of thoughtful reflection as well as of aggressive action. Educators often bemoan the supposed anti-intellectual fervor of Americans; perhaps ours is not so much an anti-intellectual culture as it is anti-reflective. We value speed and volume more than meditation and judgment. Another way of regarding seminar discussion is as the part of every unit of study that values and nurtures reflection, both in the individual and community. As Hutchins (1952) wrote years ago, the liberally educated individual "is at home . . . in the world of practical affairs" in addition to "the world of ideas . . . because he understands the relation of the two" (p. 4). In other words, the thoughtful individual can act incisively because he or she is prepared to do so by study and practice. Vigorous action flows out of reflection; cogent thought flows out of potent action. When we coach student action through product-oriented projects and coach student thought through idea-rich discussion, we teach the complementary capacities for both. When we successively integrate the seminar into the coached project, we teach active thought and thoughtful action. Once again, the key to teaching these skills effectively is our own ability to teach with judgment and energy.

3. Self-reliance as well as collaboration. The third set of complementary habits that we must teach is defined by the tension between independence and collaboration. In our new focus on communication and cooperation, we need to remember that powerful collaboration results from the synergy of potent individuals. Emerson's "sturdy lad from New Hampshire or Vermont" is above all else self-reliant (thus the title of Emerson's essay) and so "has not one chance but a hundred chances" that he makes or finds for himself. When a teacher assigns the members of a design or implementation team to a coached project or looks around a seminar circle at the participants, he or she places the highest value on variety—variety of personality, skill, and background. When Emerson writes that "the virtue in most request is conformity" and "self-reliance is its aversion," he might be describing first the traditional classroom and then the Paideia classroom (1979, p. 51).

Toward Continual Learning and Growth

In any setting where students are learning and practicing teamwork, the first lesson is that they must together value and nurture the independent skills of each so as to build the strongest team possible. Thus, it is in the seminar that individual children learn to trust their own judgment (even when it runs counter to that of others), and it is as part of a production team that they learn the value of independent hard work (as it contributes to the whole). In "grading" both the coached project and seminar participation, teachers have already learned that they must rely heavily on students working alone *and* together to assess the ongoing quality of their own work, revising their efforts as they go (see Chapter 8). Furthermore, if we are to create in our schools true learning communities, we must as adults learn to be both universally self-reliant as well as powerfully collaborative.

If we are to instill in our students a lifelong commitment to quality, we must both learn and share the profound realization that quality is a fluid measure that will increase as skills and understanding increase. In this way, as decades pass, students will become increasingly knowledgeable, increasingly skilled, and increasingly wise.

As with all the essential elements of a Paideia school, the question remains: Where have we already achieved success? We have begun to measure our success in the expanded involvement of the adult community in Cason Lane Academy (in Murfreesboro, Tennessee), in the expanded use of individual student portfolios from kindergarten through 12th grade at the Pueblo School of Arts and Sciences (in Colorado), and in the parent/community seminars at Brentmoor Elementary School (in Mentor, Ohio). We have begun to measure our growth in countless schools around the United States where teachers have redefined their classrooms as master-apprentice workshops so they can work together with their students on products of value to the larger human community.

We have achieved fragments of the 14th Essential Element in countless schools around the United States, but we have not yet achieved the kind of school where true lifelong learning is consistently modeled and nurtured. Because we have not yet achieved it, however, does not mean that we cannot now conceive and strive toward it. In the closing paragraph of

"Civil Disobedience," Henry David Thoreau (1983) describes the government that he believed would evolve out of 19th century democracy. If we substitute the word *school* for *state*, we might read his closing sentence thus:

> A *school* which bore this kind of fruit [academic excellence for all members of the community], and suffered it to drop off as fast as it ripened, would prepare the way for a still more perfect and glorious *school*, which also I have imagined, but not yet anywhere seen. (p. 413)

It is now more apparent than ever that we cannot afford to rest on our laurels in improving our schools. Cultural and social evolution waits neither for institutions nor communities. The incisive message of the 14th Essential Element—and of this entire book—is that as individuals and as communities, we must *continually* learn and *continually* grow.

APPENDIX A
GETTING STARTED

When discussing the "ideal" Paideia implementation plan, we must first stress that no two efforts are ever quite the same. Indeed, it is essential to our program (and, we believe, any successful professional development program) that participants have ongoing opportunities for involvement in the design and direction of training. Local empowerment necessitates flexibility; however, after years of addressing the varying needs of widely differing communities, we have been struck by a number of similarities that characterize the development of almost all successful Paideia schools.

When teachers, administrators, or parents become interested in Paideia school reform, they should contact the National Paideia Center for more information and arrange, if possible, to visit a Paideia school (see Appendix B). After the initial inquiry, we usually suggest an information session in which a member of the National Paideia Center staff visits the community and introduces teachers, administrators, and parents to Paideia theory and practice. If the school community generates sufficient interest, we follow this introduction with a planning and enrollment period. During this time, we involve the teachers and administrators in tailoring our staff development model to their specific needs.

We believe that there are at least two reasons for the recent success of the National Paideia Center in staff development:

1. Without exception, the members of our training staff are all former or current classroom teachers or administrators. We believe that their background gives us not only an acute awareness of the needs and concerns of teachers, but also of how professional development programs most effectively address those needs.

2. The research on professional development supports the notion that, for a reform program to be successful, teachers need to be integrally involved in its ongoing development. Clearly, then, it is to our mutual advantage to plan training and technical support programs *with* teachers and administrators, not *for* them.

Our usual pattern is to stress the use of the Paideia seminar schoolwide during the first year of a program. Three to five days of intensive training are provided for all teachers and administrators (plus interested parents) before school opens. As part of this program, we work with the staff to plan and institute a series of schoolwide seminars. These seminars, held regularly throughout the year, are based on concrete objectives for student behavior and achievement, and so allow all students and teachers ample opportunity to master their seminar skills. We follow this initial training with monthly on-site visits throughout the first year. During these visits, National Paideia Center staff

- Lead, observe, and coach the leadership of seminars;
- Address faculty concerns as they arise;
- Work with school leadership to support instruction; and
- Help establish an on-site Paideia committee that will, over the next few years, assume increasing responsibility for the program.

The training itself follows the research on successful classroom innovation (Joyce and Showers, 1989). Participants are first introduced to the *theory* behind the seminar and then participate in concrete *demonstrations*. They are then led through a series of sessions wherein they repeatedly *practice* seminar facilitation while receiving *feedback* from National Paideia Center staff. Once all participants can demonstrate the skills of seminar leadership, we help them design a classroom-based *peer coaching* model that will support their efforts throughout the first year.

After creating a successful seminar program, we use a similar training plan in the second year to implement schoolwide coached projects, and, in the third year, to create a fully functional Paideia instructional program. These systemic changes in instruction are supported by careful revisions in all areas that support instruction: scheduling, assessment, governance, community relations, to name a few. The important thing in the second and third year of the program is to engender (and, where they already exist, nurture) the ongoing development of a true learning community, wherein adults model for children their own continuing human development.

Because we focus first and last on working with teachers to directly improve student achievement, we believe we can institute a climate of academic rigor for all students and thus create true classical schools for the 21st century.

APPENDIX B
PAIDEIA SCHOOLS BY STATE

The following schools are both dedicated to becoming fully functional Paideia schools and involved in that effort with the National Paideia Center. Although these schools are at many different stages of developing systemic Paideia programs, they are all part of the larger network of mutually supportive Paideia school-communities dedicated to providing a rigorous classical education for all children. (An asterisk after a school name denotes a charter school.)

ALASKA
Chiniak School (K–8)
Box 5657 - Chiniak
Kodiak, AK 99615-5657
907-486-5500
Contact: Elaine Griffin, 1995 National Teacher of the Year

ARKANSAS
Thomas Jefferson Elementary School (K–5)
301 N.W. Third St.
Bentonville, AK 72712
501-271-1123
Contact: Galen Havner, Principal

COLORADO
Community Prep School* (9–12)
332 E. Willamette Ave.
Colorado Springs, CO 80903
719-578-5495
Contact: Ray Rodriguez, Director

Pueblo School of Arts and Sciences* (K–12)
745 Acero
Pueblo, CO 31004
719-549-2737
Contact: Sam Pantleo, Principal

South Street Elementary (K–6)
1100 South St.
Castle Rock, CO 80104
303-688-4658
Contact: Jorge-Ayn Riley, Principal

FLORIDA
Darnell-Cookman Middle School (6–8)
1701 Davis St.
Jacksonville, FL 32209
904-630-6828
Contact: Mike Budd, Principal

NOVA Center for Applied Research & Professional Development
A Cluster of Schools, K–12
3602 College Ave.
Davie, FL 33314
954-424-4124
Contact: Margarita C. Sasse, Director

ILLINOIS
Goldblatt Elementary School (K–5)
4257 W. Adams St.
Chicago, IL 60624
773-534-6860
Contact: Dhamona Shauri, Paideia Coordinator

Sullivan High School (9–12)
6631 N. Bosworth
Chicago, IL 60626
312-534-2000
Contact: Cathy Ruffalo, Principal

KENTUCKY
Williamsburg Elementary School (K–5)
1000 Main St.
Williamsburg, KY 40769
606-549-6044
Contact: Gary Pate, Principal

NEW YORK
Giblyn Elementary School (1–4)
450 S. Ocean St.
Freeport, NY 11520
516-867-5260
Contact: Tony Duhamel, Principal

Yonkers School #24 (K–3)
50 Colin St.
Yonkers, NY 10701
914-376-8640
Contact: Ellen O'Brien-Scully, Principal

NORTH CAROLINA

Schools listed in italics are part of the Guilford County, North Carolina, school system, the most active Paideia school system in the United States. For more information, contact Superintendent Jerry Weast at 910-370-8390.

Bluford Elementary School (K–5)
1901 Tuscaloosa Elementary
Greensboro, NC 27401-3839
910-370-8120
Contact: Tonya Feagins, Principal

Brown Summit Elementary (K–5)
4720 NC 150 W
Brown Summit, NC 27214-9551
910-656-4000
Contact: Sam Foust, Principal

Central Elementary School (K–5)
435 E. Stadium Dr.
Eden, NC 27288
910-623-8378
Contact: Joseph McCargo, Principal

Claxton Elementary School (K–5)
3720 Pinetop Rd.
Greensboro, NC 27410-2899
910-545-2010
Contact: Judith Dockery, Principal

Colfax Elementary School (K–5)
9112 US 421
Colfax, NC 27235-9788
910-275-4332
Contact: Linda York, Principal

Erwin Open Elementary School (K–5)
3012 E. Bessemer Ave.
Greensboro, NC 27405-7504
910-370-8150
Contact: Eunice Isley, Principal

Fairview Elementary School (K–5)
608 Fairview St.
High Point, NC 27260-4711
910-819-2945
Contact: Susan Allen, Principal

Ferndale Middle School (6–8)
701 Ferndale Boulevard
High Point, NC 27262
910-819-2900
Contact: Jules Crowell, Principal

Glen Arden Elementary (K–5)
St. John St.
Arden, NC 28704
704-684-2139
Contact: Ed Graham, Principal

Guilford Middle School (3–8)
401 College Rd.
Greensboro, NC 27410-5199
910-316-5833
Contact: Maggie Shook, Principal

Guilford Primary School (K–2)
411 Friendway Rd.
Greensboro, NC 27410-4911
910-316-5844
Contact: Dan Jones, Principal

Hawthorne Traditional Middle School (7–9)
1411 Hawthorne Lane
Charlotte, NC 28205-2923
704-343-5490
Contact: Calvin Lewers, Principal

Irving Park Elementary (K–5)
1310 Sunset Dr.
Greensboro, NC 27408-7235
910-370-8225
Contact: Robert Strong, Principal

Jamestown Middle School (6–8)
4401 Vickery Church Rd.
Jamestown, NC 27282-8913
910-819-2100
Contact: Debbie Dawson, Principal

Leland Middle School (4–8)
Old Fayetteville Rd.
Leland, NC 28451
910-371-3030
Contact: Diana Mintz, Principal

Madison Elementary School (K–5)
3600 Hines Chapel Rd.
McLeansville, NC 27301-9796
910-375-2555
Contact: Denese Byrd, Principal

Mendenhall Middle School (6–8)
205 Willoughby Blvd.
Greensboro, NC 27408-4499
910-545-2000
Contact: Terry Worrell, Principal

Millis Road Elementary (K–5)
4310 Millis Rd.
Jamestown, NC 27282-8912
910-819-2125
Contact: Lynda Williams, Principal

Murphey Traditional Academy (Pre-K–5)
2306 Ontario St.
Greensboro, NC 27403-3661
910-294-7380
Contact: Alma Stokes, Principal

Nathanael Greene Elementary School (K–5)
2717 NC 62 E
Liberty, NC 27298-9613
910-685-5000
Contact: Bill Hoke, Principal

Northwest Guilford High School (9–12)
5240 N.W. School Rd.
Greensboro, NC 27409-9798
910-605-3300
Contact: Anne Murr, Principal

Oak Hill Elementary (K–5)
320 Wrightenberry St.
Greensboro, NC 27260-1565
910-819-2925
Contact: Elaine Harris, Principal

Oak Ridge Elementary (K-5)
2050 Oak Ridge Rd.
Oak Ridge, NC 27310-9732
910-643-8410
Contact: Beverly Tucker, Principal

Paideia Academy at Oakhurst (K–6)
4511 Monroe Rd.
Charlotte, NC 28205
704-343-6482
Contact: Meryle Elko, Paideia Coordinator

Sedgefield Elementary School (K–5)
2905 Groometown Rd.
Greensboro, NC 27407-5514
910-316-5858
Contact: Ron Turbyfill, Principal

Seventy-First Classical Middle School (6–8)
6830 Raeford Rd.
Fayetteville, NC 28304
910-864-0092
Contact: Joann Pearce, Principal

Southeast Guilford Middle School (6–8)
4825 Woody Mill Rd.
Greensboro, NC 27406-9767
910-674-4280
Contact: Sue Jones, Principal

Union Cross Elementary School (K–5)
4300 High Point Rd.
Kernersville, NC 27284
910-769-9031
Contact: Vincent Parker, Principal

Washington Park Primary School (K–5)
1225 S. Caledonia Rd.
Laurenburg, NC 28352
910-277-4364
Contact: Beth Ammons, Principal

OHIO

Underlining denotes schools that are part of the Cincinnati network of magnet Paideia schools. Contact Magnet Coordinator Robert Townsend at 513-475-7000 for more information.

Brentmoor Elementary School (K–6)
7671 Johnnycake Rd.
Mentor, OH
216-255-7813
Contact: Tim Tatko, Principal

Carthage Paideia Elementary (K–6)
125 W. Northbend
Cincinnati, OH 45216
513-482-4830
Contact: Nancy Colgrove, Principal

Eastwood Paideia School (K–6)
5030 Duck Creek Rd.
Cincinnati, OH 45227
513-533-6580
Contact: Benny Miles, Principal

Hughes Center (9–12)
2515 Clifton Ave.
Cincinnati, OH 45219
513-559-3000
Contact: Robert Seuss, Principal

Jacobs Center (7–8)
5425 Winton Ridge Lane
Cincinnati, OH 45232
513-853-6750
Contact: Stephanie Morton, Principal

Roberts Paideia Academy (K–8)
1700 Grand Ave.
Cincinnati, OH 45214
513-244-3040
Contact: Sarah Helm, Paideia Coordinator

Rockdale Paideia Elementary School (K–6)
305 Rockdale
Cincinnati, OH 45229
513-872-7950
Contact: Louise Stevenson, Principal

Shroder Paideia School (7–8)
3500 Lumford Pl.
Cincinnati, OH 45213
513-458-2040
Contact: Raymond Spicer, Principal

Silverton Paideia School (K–6)
6829 Stewart Rd.
Cincinnati, OH 45236
513-458-2070
Contact: Henri Bradshaw, Principal

Woodford Paideia Elementary School (K–6)
6065 Red Bank Rd.
Cincinnati, OH 45213
513-458-2060
Contact: Jetta King, Paideia Facilitator

TENNESSEE

Cason Lane Academy (K–8)
1330 Cason Ln.
Murfreesboro, TN 37129
615-898-7145
Contact: Susan Gendrich-Cameron, Principal

Chattanooga School of Arts and Sciences (K–12)
865 E. Third St.
Chattanooga, TN 37403
615-757-5495
Contact: Susan Martin, Visitor Coordinator

Fairview Junior High School (7–9)
750 E. Parkway St.
Memphis, TN 38113
901-722-4536
Contact: Charles Earle, Principal

Phoenix School #3 (9–12)
1301 Dallas Rd.
Chattanooga, TN 37405
923-757-5002
Contact: Joanne Smith, Principal

Richland Elementary School (K–6)
5440 Rich Rd.
Memphis, TN 38120
901-684-2148
Contact: Joyce Jensen, Principal

Trezevant Junior and Senior High School (7–12)
3350 Trezevant St.
Memphis, TN 38127
901-375-3767
Contact: Ann Herron, Principal

VIRGINIA
Patrick Henry High School (9–12)
12449 W. Patrick Henry Rd.
Ashland, VA 23005
804-752-6023
Contact: Chris Lundberg, Assistant Principal

WASHINGTON
Woodbrook Middle School (6–8)
14920 Spring St., S.W.
Tacoma, WA 98439
206-589-7680
Contact: Karen Hansen, Principal

APPENDIX C
ASSESSMENT TOOLS

Section I: Coached Project Checklist

The following checklist is for assessing the degree to which a coached project is being successfully implemented in a classroom. (Note that the sophistication of students' responses will vary with their ages.) This checklist is intended for use by administrators and teachers who have been trained by the National Paideia Center staff in product-oriented coached projects. It is for use as an assessment of the ongoing process, not as a teacher evaluation tool.

Questions to Ask the Teacher:
1. Can the teacher explain clearly how the project aligns with the curriculum goals for which he or she and the students are responsible?

YES _____   NO _____

2. Can the teacher describe in some detail the nature of the final product and its relevance to students?

YES _____   NO _____

3. Can the teacher describe how students were involved in choosing and designing the product?

YES _____   NO _____

Environmental Observations:
4. Are the classroom furniture and equipment arranged to facilitate the creation of the product in question?

YES _____   NO _____

5. Are there recognizable "centers" or work stations in the room dedicated to the production of various elements of the final product?

YES _____   NO _____

6. Is a representation of the finished product displayed in the classroom?

YES _____   NO _____

7. Is a calendar of learning events leading up to the finished product displayed in the classroom?

YES _____   NO _____

8. Is a rubric available for judging the quality of the final product?

YES _____   NO _____

9. Do the students in the classroom appear to be working successfully in teams?

YES _____   NO _____

10. Are the majority of students in the classroom at work?

YES _____   NO _____

Questions to Ask Several Students:
(Select different students at random for each question.)
11. Can students describe the end product of the project on which they are engaged?

YES _____   NO _____

12. Can students explain how they were involved in the creation of the final product rubric?

YES _____   NO _____

13. Can students explain how their current work will lead to the creation of the end product or contribute to its quality?

YES _____   NO _____

14. Can students describe decisions that they individually or as members of a group had to make as part of the project?

YES _____   NO _____

15. Can students describe the skills they must master in order to guarantee the quality of the final product?

YES _____   NO _____

16. Can a student jot down the names of a significant number of other students and adults that they had to work closely with as part of the project?

YES _____   NO _____

17. Does that list contain a wide variety of individuals?

YES _____   NO _____

18. Can students explain clearly how their work will be evaluated and how the evaluation will be recorded and reported?

YES _____   NO _____

19. Can students describe the processes by which their work habits are periodically assessed and revised?

YES _____   NO _____

20. Do they feel they were involved in the assessment process?

YES _____   NO _____

21. Can students explain the significance of the end product:

as evidence of what they have learned?

YES _____   NO _____

to themselves as individuals?

YES _____   NO _____

to the world outside the school?

YES _____   NO _____

Section II: Chattanooga School of Arts and Sciences Seminar Evaluation Rubric[1]

Name _____ Grade Level _____

Facilitator(s) _____ Date _____

Evaluation Areas/Outcomes

Critical Reading:

0	1	2	3	4
Non-scoreable	Beginning	Developing	Very Good	Exemplary

Listening:

0	1	2	3	4
Non-scoreable	Beginning	Developing	Very Good	Exemplary

Reasoning:

0	1	2	3	4
Non-scoreable	Beginning	Developing	Very Good	Exemplary

Speaking:

0	1	2	3	4
Non-scoreable	Beginning	Developing	Very Good	Exemplary

Writing:

0	1	2	3	4
Non-scoreable	Beginning	Developing	Very Good	Exemplary

Comments:

---

[1]The Chattanooga School of Arts and Sciences Seminar Evaluation Rubric is reprinted with the permission of Julie McAloon, Marcy Anderson, and the Chattanooga School of Arts and Sciences Seminar Committee.

(continued)

	4 Exemplary	3 Very Good	2 Developing	1 Beginning	0 Non-scoreable
Critical Reading	• Clearly addresses focus (assignment) for critical reading	• Addresses focus for critical reading	• Attempts to address focus for critical reading	• Ineffectively addresses focus for critical reading	• Fails to address focus for critical reading
Listening	• References previous remarks • Directs comments/ questions to others • Demonstrates appropriate listening behaviors (eye contact, waiting until another is finished before speaking, etc.)	• References previous remarks • Directs comments to others • Aware of appropriate listening behaviors	• Sometimes references previous remarks • Occasionally directs comments to others • Inconsistently demonstrates appropriate listening behaviors	• Rarely makes reference to previous remarks • Rarely directs comments to others • Rarely demonstrates appropriate listening behaviors	• No reference made to previous remarks • Fails to address other participants • Demonstrates inappropriate listening behaviors
Reasoning	• Comments are timely and relevant to discussion • Comments/questions move discussion beyond surface content, address complex ideas • Provides clear support from text and other examples • Comments are timely and relevant	• Comments make connections to previous ideas/occasionally questions • Responses move discussion beyond surface/occasionally questions • Provides support from text or other examples • Comments relevant/sometimes timely	• Attempts to make connections/no questioning • Attempts understanding/no questioning • Provides support occasionally through examples • Comments may be relevant, but not timely	• Can respond to questions that make connections • Restates previous remarks/ideas • Provides support with prompting	• Comments irrelevant and untimely • No connections made • Only stays at surface • Does not provide support for ideas

(continued)

	4 Exemplary	3 Very Good	2 Developing	1 Beginning	0 Non-scoreable
Speaking	• Speaks at an appropriate pace and volume • Uses vocabulary appropriate to ideas expressed • Uses correct grammar • Organizes ideas as speaking	• Speaks at an appropriate pace/volume may be coached • Uses vocabulary appropriate to ideas/occasional coaching needed • Uses correct grammar • Usually able to organize as speaking	• Speaks at an appropriate pace/can be heard most of the time • With coaching, vocabulary appropriate to ideas expressed • Incorrect grammar and distracting to listeners • Ideas unorganized, but listener can understand what is being conveyed	• Speaks at an appropriate pace and volume when prompted by others • Vocabulary not on appropriate level • Incorrect grammar distracts listener from ideas presented • Rambles/ideas unorganized	• Cannot be heard
Writing	• Addresses focus for assignment • Reflects clear organizational plan (smooth progression) • Offers examples that clearly support main idea • No errors in grammar or mechanics	• Addresses focus for assignment • Reflects organizational plan (good progression) • Offers relevant examples in support of main idea • Few errors in grammar or mechanics	• Attempts to address focus for assignment • Reflects some organization • Occasionally offers relevant examples in support of main idea • Errors in grammar and mechanics not distracting	• Ineffectively addresses focus for assignment • Reflects incomplete organization • Offers vague/ irrelevant examples for support • Errors in grammar and mechanics distract the reader	• Fails to address focus for assignment • Lacks organization (no progression) • No examples offered for support

Section III: Seminar Teaching Guide[1]

This instrument can be used by teachers for self-assessment, by administrators and other colleagues to determine teacher effectiveness, and by trainers when instructing new learners. It is designed to provide information and guidance in areas that can be improved, and the observer using the instrument should provide suggestions to the teacher for improvement. The seminar leader can be videotaped conducting a seminar, and afterward the individual can view the video alone or with another colleague using the instrument to determine areas for improvement.

Part 1 of the instrument is a checklist with space between the items for specific comments about those items. The teacher can use that space to explain why a behavior occurred or did not occur, and the observer can note suggestions for improvement or provide examples of the behavior that occurred. Part 2 is a short-answer portion that the teacher can fill in before self-evaluation or talking with an administrator or another colleague.

In some cases the items will contain an AND. The observer should be aware of this and note that mastering one portion of the item does not necessarily mean that item has been satisfactorily completed. The observer should write in the space provided explaining which parts of the item were done satisfactorily and which were not.

As you complete the instrument, please keep in mind the purpose of the "Seminar Teaching Guide" is to provide guidance and feedback (not only by other individuals but also for self-assessment) on the conduct of the seminar. The instrument is a profile with suggestions for improvement. It is not designed to yield a score that could be used to rank or rate the performance of the teacher. All of the items are not equally important, and a ranking would not be beneficial.

Training is necessary before using the instrument to provide specific, helpful recommendations to teachers and to make sure the items are interpreted as intended.

---

[1]Excerpted from Amy Bender's Ph.D. dissertation, "Paideia Seminar Teaching Guide: An Assessment Instrument to Identify Skills for Effective Teachers," completed at the Department of Education, University of North Carolina at Chapel Hill in 1994. It is reprinted here with her permission.

The teacher should attach a copy of the questions prepared for use during the seminar.

—Amy Bender
A former staff member of the National Paideia Center

Name _____

Grade Level _____

Subject _____

Part 1

Preparation for Seminar

	Yes	No
1. Text[2] chosen was appropriate for a seminar AND the age of the students.	_____	_____
2. The room was set up so that participants could make eye contact with one another (e.g., circle or square).	_____	_____
3. Teacher had clearly stated expectations for behavior as evidenced by the students' actions.	_____	_____

Teacher as Facilitator

4. Teacher was seated on the same level as the students in the seminar.	_____	_____
5. Teacher was knowledgeable about the text being discussed AND could locate references in the text quickly.	_____	_____
6. Teacher refrained from giving his or her own opinion during the seminar.	_____	_____
7. Teacher encouraged student interaction (listening as well as speaking) by keeping track of those who spoke, providing opportunities for shy students, asking follow-up questions, AND asking students to respond to what had been said.	_____	_____

---

[2]Throughout this instrument the word *text* is used to mean a primary source material such as a document, short story, piece of art work, play, music, and so forth.

	Yes	No
8. Teacher guided students when they made factual errors by further questioning or probing if they were not corrected by other students.	_____	_____
9. Teacher asked for clarification AND connections between ideas.	_____	_____
10. Teacher brought students back to the text when they digressed.	_____	_____
11. Teacher kept one or two students from dominating or monopolizing the conversation.	_____	_____
12. Teacher kept the seminar participants from arguing out of control.	_____	_____
13. Teacher occasionally paraphrased students' remarks when necessary.	_____	_____
14. Teacher stopped misbehavior quickly AND effectively if students made no effort to curb one another's inappropriate behavior.	_____	_____
15. Teacher accepted, encouraged, AND supported divergent views and opinions.	_____	_____
16. Teacher included the whole group in the discussion AND did not focus on only a few members of the group.	_____	_____
17. Teacher's body language AND facial expressions were accepting of all students.	_____	_____

	Yes	No

18. Teacher refrained from providing traditional closure for the students by summarizing at the end of the seminar. _____ _____

Questioning Strategies

19. Opening question was broad, AND each participant was given an opportunity to respond. _____ _____

20. Teacher was a good listener AND framed follow-up questions from student comments. _____ _____

21. Teacher asked questions that generated higher-order thinking (synthesis, analysis, or evaluation) responses from the students. _____ _____

22. Teacher asked questions that encouraged students to explore relevance of text to their present lives. _____ _____

23. Teacher allowed sufficient wait-time for students to think before the students responded or another question was asked. _____ _____

24. Questions posed did not lead the students to a preconceived "right" answer. _____ _____

25. Teacher made smooth transitions between questions asked. _____ _____

26. Teacher questioned students, not telling or teaching factual knowledge about the text. _____ _____

Student Participation

	Yes	No
27. Students had a copy of the text being discussed in front of them.	___	___
28. Students observed the rules of seminar participation (put chairs in circle, met expectations for behavior).	___	___
29. Students talked more than the teacher.	___	___
30. Students did not require permission (from the teacher or other students) to speak during the seminar.	___	___
31. Students directed their comments to one another rather than the teacher.	___	___
32. Students showed respect for others' views and opinions by listening AND by not criticizing other students for differing responses.	___	___
33. Students supported their statements with references to the text.	___	___
34. Students used one another's names when agreeing or disagreeing with other students.	___	___
35. Students asked questions during the seminar.	___	___
36. Students were comfortable sharing opinions based on text evidenced by a conversation-like atmosphere.	___	___

Part 2

This portion of the instrument is designed to give the teacher an opportunity to reflect on the seminar and to provide additional information to the observer that may make a difference in the observation. Please answer the following questions as specifically as possible at the bottom of the page or attach additional pages to the end of this instrument.

- I have led _____ (approximate number) seminars this year with this class.

- Were you comfortable leading this seminar? Are there any special circumstances that should be considered by a person observing who has not been in your class every day?

- How does this seminar text fit into your lesson plans?

- What did you do to prepare the students for the seminar (preseminar activities, coaching, or didactic instruction)?

- What kind of follow-up activities are planned for the students?

- How do you determine student understanding of the seminar?

- After completing this observation, what areas of your seminar leading do you feel need improvement?

- Additional Comments or Questions:

BIBLIOGRAPHY

Adler, M. (1982). *The Paideia proposal*. New York: Macmillan.

Adler, M. (1983). *Paideia problems and possibilities*. New York: Macmillan.

Adler, M. (1984). *The Paideia program*. New York: Macmillan.

Adler, M. (1996). On multiculturalism. *Philosophy Is Everybody's Business, 3*(2), 8–28.

Bloom, B.S., Engelhart, M.D., Furst, E.J., Hill, W.H., & Krathwohl, D.R. (1956). *Taxonomy of educational objectives: Handbook I: Cognitive domain*. New York: David McKay.

Carey, J. (1987). *Eyewitness to history*. Cambridge: Harvard University Press.

Darling-Hammond, L. (1996). The right to learn and the advancement of teaching: Research, policy, and practice for democratic education. *Educational Researcher, 25*(6), 5–17.

Down, A. G. (1996). The three assassins of excellence. *Education Week 16*(5), 35.

Down, A. G. (n.d.). Phone conversation with Gail Gellatly.

Earl, L.M., & LeMahieu, P.G. (1997). Rethinking assessment and accountability. In A. Hargreaves (Ed.), *Rethinking educational change with heart and mind: 1997 ASCD yearbook* (pp. 149–168). Alexandria, VA: ASCD.

Emerson, R. W. (1979). Self-reliance. *The collected works of Ralph Waldo Emerson*. Vol. 2. Cambridge, MA: Belknap Press of Harvard University Press.

Gardner, H. (1983). *Frames of mind: The theory of multiple intelligences*. New York: Basic Books.

Gray, D. (1984, March).Whatever became of Paideia? *Educational Leadership, 42*(6), 56–57.

Hirsch, E. D. (1987). *Cultural literacy*. New York: Houghton Mifflin.

Hutchins, R., (Ed.). (1952). *The great conversation*. Vol. 1 of *Great books of the Western world*. Chicago: Encyclopaedia Britannica.

Joyce, B., & Showers, B. (1989, November). School renewal as cultural change. *Educational Leadership, 47*(3), 70–77.

McDonald, J.P., Smith, S., Turner, D., Finney, M., & Barton, E. (1993). *Graduation by exhibition: Assessing genuine achievement*. Alexandria, VA: ASCD.

Messick, S. (1994). The interplay of evidence and consequences in the validation of performance assessments. *Educational Researcher, 23*(2), 13–23.

Miller, E. (1994, November/December). A slap on the heart: teachers' expectations and kids' achievement in the arts. *The Harvard Education Letter*, 7–8.

National Commission on Excellence in Education. (1983). *A nation at risk: The imperative for educational reform*. Washington, DC: U.S. Government Printing Office.

National Education Commission on Time and Learning. (1994). *Prisoners of time*. Washington, D.C.: Author.

National Paideia Center. (1988). The Paideia principles. Unpublished handout.

Noddings, N. (1992). *The challenge to care in schools*. New York: Teachers College Press.

Ravitch, D. (1983). The proposal in perspective. *Harvard Educational Review*, (53)4, 380–383.

Sawchick, C. (1995). Art represents, science explains. *Paideia Next Century*, 4(3), 4.

Secretary's Commission on Achieving Necessary Skills. (1991). *What work requires of schools: A SCANS report for America 2000*. Washington, DC: U.S. Department of Labor.

Thoreau, H. (1983). Civil disobedience. In *Walden and civil disobedience*. New York: Penguin.

Van Doren, J. (1984). Fine arts. In M. Adler (Ed.), *The Paideia program*. New York: Macmillan.

Vincent, P. (1994). *Developing character in students*. Chapel Hill, NC: New View Publications.

Wheelock, A. (1992). *Crossing the tracks: How "untracking" can save America's schools*. New York: The New Press.

Wheelock, A. (1994). Chattanooga's Paideia schools: A single track for all—and it's working. *Journal of Negro Education*, 63(1), 77–92.

White, T. H. (1939). *The once and future king*. New York: Putnam.

Wiggins, G. (1993). *Assessing student performance: Exploring the purpose and limits of testing*. San Francisco: Jossey-Bass.

Wood, G. (1992). *Schools that work: America's most innovative public education programs*. New York: Plume.

INDEX

Page numbers followed by "*f*" refer to figures.

ABOUT THE AUTHORS

Terry Roberts is the Executive Director of the National Paideia Center at the University of North Carolina at Greensboro. A former high school English teacher and an American literature scholar, he brings to school reform the passion of a devoted teacher as well as the conviction that intellectual rigor is the birthright of every American child. He has written widely on teaching and learning and, with his colleagues at the Paideia Center, works on a daily basis with schools across the United States.

As is wholly appropriate for a book about the common cause of classical learning, the production of *The Power of Paideia Schools: Defining Lives Through Learning* was a profoundly collaborative act. And like Terry Roberts, the other staff at the National Paideia Center who were involved in the book's creation are all former teachers and principals dedicated to the practical application of the ideal.

Laura Billings is the Assistant Director of Curriculum and Instruction at the National Paideia Center. She is the former Director of the Cities and Schools Program at Andrew Jackson High School in Jacksonville, Florida, as well as an experienced junior and senior high school English teacher. She is particularly interested in the seminar as democratic dialogue and authentic assessment in the Paideia classroom.

William Chesser is a former Assistant Director of Training and Outreach at the National Paideia Center currently involved in the development of educational software. He is also a former middle and high school English teacher who is interested in the seminar K–12.

Gail Gellatly is an Assistant Director of Operations at the National Paideia Center. A former Montessori Director, she has a special interest in the arts in education and developed and taught art programs for children at the School of the Art Institute in Chicago.

Michael Hale is Senior Program Associate at the National Paideia Center. He is a former high school social studies teacher. His research interests involve school change, professional development, and the structural context of teaching.

Lois Johnson is a former Assistant Director of Training and Outreach at the National Paideia Center. She is a former middle school principal from Jacksonville, Florida, who was involved in starting the Paideia program at Darnell-Cookman Middle School.

The authors can be reached at:

National Paideia Center
School of Education
University of North Carolina at Greensboro
P.O. Box 26171
Greensboro, NC 27402-6171
http://www.unc.edu/paideia/